Am I
Who I Am?

Am I
Who I Am?

The Identity
of Jesus Confirmed

PHILIP E. LINDBERG

Pleasant W rd
A Division of WINEPRESS PUBLISHING

Pleasant Word (a division of WinePress Publishing, PO Box 428, Enumclaw, WA 98022) functions only as book publisher. As such, the ultimate design, content, editorial accuracy, and views expressed or implied in this work are those of the author.

Unless otherwise noted, all Scriptures are taken from the New King James Version®. Copyright © 1982 by Thomas Nelson, Inc. Used by permission.

The italics or underline used in Scripture quotations is the discretion of the author for the purpose of emphasizing key words or phrases.

ISBN 13: 978-1-4141-0906-0
ISBN 10: 1-4141-0906-7
Library of Congress Catalog Card Number: 2006910524

Dedication

I AM

I am who I am;
I lived before Abraham.
My thoughts are not yours to take;
My ways you cannot make.
I'm called Creator of the universe,
Alpha and Omega; Keeper of the earth.
For I am The Holy One,
My limit is beyond infinity's run.
I am the Light of the world; I created darkness too,
The Way, the Truth, the Life, the only hope for you.
My law shall stand through eternity and beyond
the farthest star;
I am unlimited in time, place, power, and
knowledge from afar.
I am the Messiah, Monarch, Ruler, and King;
No one was before Me; I am the Mainspring.
I am here, there, everywhere, the high command,
I rule the sea, sky, sun, moon, stars, and land.
I lay down My life that I may take it again;
Only I have the power of death and life herein.
I am Almighty God to the nth degree;
I am who I am; I am He.

—PHILIP FREEMAN LINDBERG (1926-2001)

Table of Contents

Acknowledgments

I honestly don't know how this book would have been completed without the help of my son, Tim. I called him on every computer problem or question I had, be it big or small. He was always available either after work or on a rare day off. May God bless him for his expertise and patience!

Joy (my wife) graciously gave me all the time and privacy I needed and yet was always there when I needed advice or an opinion on a moment's notice. God has blessed her with common sense, wisdom and logic.

Chapter One

How Could God Not Exist?

A question that is often asked, is "Does God exist"? The real question should be "How could God not exist"?

> The heavens declare the glory of God; And the firmament shows His handiwork.
>
> —Ps. 19:1

> For every house is built by someone, but He who built all things is God.
>
> —Heb. 3:4

God has promised to prove His existence to every person who will genuinely seek Him.

> The Lord is near to all who call upon Him.
>
> —Ps. 145:18

> Draw near to God and He will draw near to
> you.
>
> —James 4:8

God accomplishes this promise every day! One of God's many methods of accomplishment is in the book He wrote. A best seller! We call His book the Bible. The Bible is also referred to as "the Word of God." God has much to say about Himself in His book and the book you are now reading relies heavily on hundreds of Scriptures from the Bible, focusing on who God is. The more you know about God, the more you know about yourself. The more you know about yourself, the more you understand your need for God.

We don't have the answers to many of life's questions, but I do know who does—the only true and wise God of the Bible. He knows! He can be trusted! God loves us and He has a plan for us that is fantastically glorious. That plan will exist for all of eternity. However, right now your best, most intelligent guess of what God's eternity might be is…well, less likely than a garden full of earth worms putting their heads together and building a life-sustaining rocket ship that is capable of flying to all the stars in the universe.

God is saying to all believers, stretch your imaginations to the best of what you think heaven could be, but you won't even be close. Personally, I think we will be able to travel anywhere in the universe, visit billions of planets, and travel at the speed of instant thought (the speed of light would be too slow!). God's answer to me—you are thinking like a worm. What I have planned is, well…you are just going to have to wait and see, for…

> "Eye has not seen, nor ear heard, nor have entered into the heart of man the things which God has prepared for those who love Him."
>
> —1 Cor. 2:9

In His book (the Bible) God is speaking to all people of all races in all times. The answers we really need are there.

> "Seek and you will find; knock and it will be opened to you."
>
> —Luke 7:9-10

> "Declaring the end from the beginning, and from ancient times things that are not yet done."
>
> —Isa. 46:10

The Bible is the most popular book ever sold (and printed) in the world, year after year. It is the most published book of all time, whether religious or secular. It is so far ahead of all other books, there is no contest, yet it is never included on the best seller lists. (I wonder why?) No book ever has or ever will compare to the Bible. Why? Because the Bible is the inspired Word of the one and only true God. God always tells the truth. His prophesies are, and always will be, 100% correct. God is never wrong. Are you willing to listen? It is a choice, you know!

Chapter Two

Have You Read the Book?

Yes, I'm referring to the Bible. I am not judging or criticizing, just asking. Can you remember in your childhood believing, or wondering, if God even existed? Has that opinion changed one way or the other, now that you are an adult? Did you go to church very much as a child, or now as an adult? As for me, as far back as I can remember, I always believed in God. I am not sure why, except of course, I now know that God first loved me. I guess a little exposure was enough to accept that there must be a God. I assumed that believing God existed and making some effort to be good would be enough to go to heaven at the end of my life here on earth. I discovered however, that my effort embarrassingly fell short!

If you have never actually read the Bible, do you pretty much think you know what it says? I believe many people think they have a reasonably good idea as to what the Bible is about, even though they have not really read it. Things like, in the beginning God created the heavens and the earth. The flood and Noah's ark. The ten commandments (can't name all of them, but there are a lot of DO NOT'S). Jesus was born. Jesus performed some miracles. Jesus died on a cross (that was sadistic and abusive, but why did they have to kill Him?). Good people, like you and me, go to heaven, right? Bad people go to hell. We all can say amen to that! God decides who goes where, so let's just leave the rest of the Bible to preachers and Christian schools. Well OK, if a person wants to read and study the Bible, that's their business, but it is best if they keep it to themselves. Nobody wants religion pushed on them.

Well, that was all I thought I needed to know about God and the Bible, so why read it? It will all work out; besides I did not need to be a religious fanatic about a book. After all, it is a very big book. Most of it is probably boring or over my head and it was written thousands of years ago.

One day someone asked me if I had ever actually read the Bible. Honestly, I had read bits and pieces, but no, I had never really read the Bible. He said "try starting in the New Testament and read every chapter; you will be impressed." I don't know why, but I did. I read every chapter and I was impressed! Wow, it was actually fun to read, much different than I had assumed. How about that, I actually understood some of what I was reading. I read from Matthew to Revelation and enjoyed it so much, that I started over at Matthew and read it again. I thought the Bible was a great book to read just for the enjoyment of reading. Actually, I thought anyone who had not read the Bible would be surprised as to how well it was written. Christian, non-Christian, believe in God, don't believe in God, it didn't matter, just read it! Why? Because It was entertaining, it had a good story line, and it was uniquely different.

Whether I realized it or not at the time, God was communicating with me. After all, it was His book, written for me (and you). So, I read the New Testament through two and a half times, and up to that point, pretty much missed who Jesus really was and what He did for me. I really did enjoy reading the Bible though. I was impressed with Jesus, but why? There is no doubt that He was the same as other men in some ways, yet uniquely different from any man who ever lived! He was a leader and a teacher. The guy people wanted to see. People followed Him everywhere He went. They wanted to see Him perform miracles. Everyone wanted to hear His words of wisdom. He had power to heal the sick and the deformed. Jesus really loved people and demonstrated compassion for them His whole life. Yes, He could be blunt at times when someone needed to hear the truth. Nevertheless, He was really a people person. He did many miracles, and I suppose we could say, show-off miracles, but always miracles that benefited people. He told many great stories and seemed to have wisdom beyond His age. He knew the future. He was an intelligent man. He never seemed to lose a debate and always had the best answers for any situation.

At first the Bible was just a good book to read. I did not know how personal God wanted His word to mean to me. Then, God started to finally get through my slow mental comprehension and open up His truth. God chose the Bible to overwhelmingly convince me that His way is the only way, His truth is the only truth, and His will for my life is eternal life in His kingdom. God wanted me to know Jesus Christ. Trust Jesus Christ. Love Jesus Christ. I needed to know who Jesus Christ was to the best of my human capability.

Throughout the Old Testament and the New Testament, *the identity of Jesus is confirmed.* A Man, yes! Born in a stable, yes! He ate food, walked on water, talked about the Kingdom of God, yes! Died on a cross and bled real human blood, yes! But, how much does the Bible say about this Man, Jesus, eternally existing as God Almighty as well? A lot more than I can put in this book! The purpose of this book *AM I WHO I AM?* is to leave no doubts as to the Deity of Jesus Christ. His identity will be so clearly explained that anyone can choose to believe this eternal truth—"Jesus is truly God!" This book may or may not be easy to read and understand, depending on your Christian background. I do however, recommend you read it twice before you pass it on. If you already believe Jesus is God, this book will help you understand why you believe what you believe. If you are not sure, or think the Bible does not teach that Jesus is God, hold on and prepare to meet the truth God is about to reveal to you.

Today, we have easy access to God's truth and yet we have people who by choice are rejecting this truth and are trying to lead us away from Jesus. Jesus has been kicked out of our schools, government, work, sports, and some churches. And guess what? Jesus is even being eliminated from "Christmas" (and all other Christian holidays). Some companies forbid employees to say "Merry Christmas," and the Christmas tree lots say "xmas trees" or "Joe's tree lot" or just "trees." I am not implying that Christmas trees are biblical or even Christian. Also, I am not implying that it is wrong to say "happy holidays" or "seasons greetings" but rather that we are being manipulated to accept that "Jesus is NOT the reason for the season." The day Jesus was born is not so important. What is important is that He *was* born. The retail stores, public schools, and Christmas cards say "happy holidays," "seasons greetings," "winter break," "Santa Claus," etc. Anything is OK except "Jesus" or "Christ." This is spiritual warfare and you and I are in a war zone of subtle deception! So, not only at the Christmas holidays, but...

"In all your ways acknowledge Him."
—Prov. 3:6

Feel free to hug "Frosty the snowman" if that is your thing, but praise God for providing the snow! Celebrate the birth of Jesus every day, not just Dec. 25th.

Many families and friends do not discuss politics or religion. Actually, politics can be carefully mentioned, but you are on thin ice. Jesus is the one left out of most conversations!

Jesus is the most important subject in this world and no self-aware life-form ever created is more conscious of that fact than Satan! Satan is the master of deception and a liar. He makes the truth look like a lie and a lie look like the truth. He hates God and he hates you! His total focus is the *damnnation* of every member of the human race.

Only JESUS CHRIST can defeat Satan!
Only JESUS CHRIST has defeated Satan!

The Bible not only tells us how the world started, it also tells us how it will end. Actually, the earth will not end, but rather, end as we know it. God is going to do a major overhaul by eliminating sin, death, suffering, pollution, and most important, our biggest enemy, Satan. Praise the Lord!

The last book of the Bible (Revelation) is not an easy read. However, the last three chapters (20–22) explain where we are headed and how life will change, so if you haven't read it, put it on your reading list. God's Word is 100% spot-on because He knows the future and proclaims to us that His

Word has never been wrong. Try as some men might, none have ever proved the Bible wrong! It will not be wrong as far as the future is concerned either. I am sure God is pleased anytime we jump to the back of His book to read and re-read those last encouraging words. God wants us to know that He has already won the war against sin and death, and we are invited to join in and celebrate His victory with Him. How can anyone refuse this gift of eternal life?

Chapter Three

Is There More Than One God?

The main theme of the Bible is the redemption of mankind, and that redemption is by the way of the cross—the sacrifice of the blood of Jesus, who is the Christ, the Savior to all who believe. Jesus is the one and only way to eternal life. The love of God is hard to comprehend, but simple to accept. A child does not comprehend the love of a good parent, but is willing and eager to accept it. We can be God's children and not totally understand God's love. However we can know that God does love us and we can choose to be willing to accept it!

So, who is this God and what does He have to say about Himself and eternal life? God says in His Word, over and over, in both the Old Testament and New Testament, that there is *one* God, that He has always existed and He always will exist—all-knowing, all-powerful, and the Creator of all things.

"for I am God, and *there is no other;* I am God, and *there is none like Me.*"

—Isa. 46:9

"I am the Lord and there is no other; *there is no God besides Me.*"

—Isa. 45:5

"is there a God besides Me? I know not one."

—Isa. 44:8

"And understand that I am He. Before Me there was no God formed, nor shall there be after Me."

—Isa. 43:10

"To you it was shown, that you might know that the *Lord Himself* is God; *there is none other besides Him.*"

—Deut. 4:35

"the *Lord Himself is God* in heaven above and on the earth beneath; *there is no other.*"

—Deut. 4:39

"*one God* and Father of all, who is above all..."

—Eph. 4:6

"For there is *one God...*"

—1 Tim. 2:5

"Yet for us there is *one God...*"

—1 Cor. 8:6

According to the Bible (both Old and New Testament), any religion, any faith, any person that does not proclaim the God of the Bible as the one and only true God, it is false! That may seem narrow-minded and not very tolerant of other opinions and beliefs, but if the God of the Bible does exist, it seems most likely He would know if there were any other gods. If God does not know of any other gods and He knows everything, then I for one, trust the God of the Bible!

These Scriptures are only a few examples in the Bible that tell us that there is only one eternal God! Do you believe (100%) what the Bible says? If not, read on anyway, because the Bible just might be *the book* your heart, mind, and soul has been searching for. If you do believe the Bible is true, you either already have eternal life or you are on the path that leads to eternal life.

So, is this one and only God of the Bible knowable? What does He expect of us? Who can explain God? Actually, Jesus Christ had more to say about God than any man on this earth, past, present, and future. And just who might Jesus be? Why should we listen to Him? Does this one God of the Bible want us to listen to Jesus? Was Jesus really on this earth? Yes, there is more documented proof that Jesus was on this earth than even George Washington.

(God speaking)..."This is My beloved Son (Jesus), in whom I am well pleased. Hear Him!"

—Matt. 17:5

"And suddenly a voice came from heaven, saying, this is My beloved Son, in whom I am well pleased."

—Matt. 3:17

"But when the fullness of the time had come, *God sent forth His Son*...to redeem those who were under the law..."

—Gal. 4:4-5

And we have seen and testify that the *Father has sent the Son* as Savior of the world.

—1 John 4:14

Obviously, God the Father is pleased with Jesus the Son and tells us to listen to Him! And Jesus has much to say. Just check in with Matthew, Mark, Luke, and John. Jesus spoke in love to mankind, but never tried to soften the truth.

The truth is, there is a train coming (faster and faster) straight toward us. Satan is the train, and we are on the track. The light on the train is Satan's great lie and it is blinding us from the truth. We are fascinated by this light and we are curious about this light. We think we are on another track and are not afraid of the train. But there is a train on another track as well. Then as we look around, there are many trains and many tracks and we cannot see a way out of danger. Jesus knows the way out. He knows the truth about the train and the track we are really on. He says to us, let Me take your hand and I will lead you to safety, away from all the train tracks that lead to death. If you ask Jesus to take your hand, He will take it and not let go.

> "And I give them eternal life, and they shall never perish; neither shall anyone snatch them out of My hand."
>
> —John 10:28

> But Jesus took him by the hand and lifted him up....
>
> —Mark 9:27

> So He took the blind man by the hand and led him out of the town.
>
> —Mark 8:23

> But when he (Peter) saw that the wind was boisterous, he was afraid; and beginning to sink he cried out, saying, "Lord, save me!" And immediately Jesus stretched out His hand and caught him....
>
> —Matt. 14: 30-31

The most powerful hands in the universe belong to Jesus! Those hands demonstrate and communicate love, compassion, forgiveness, truth, and security! Those hands want your permission to hold on to your hand and never let go!

A side note to Mr. "macho" man. A real man knows when to lend a helping hand and when to humbly accept a helping hand when needed. We all experience both situations. It's OK to ask for directions, especially if people's lives are affected by your decisions. The hands of Jesus will not embarrass you!

Chapter Four

Is There More Than One Savior?

Who does the Bible say is the Savior of all mankind? Are you trusting in a Savior for eternal life? If so, Who is your Savior? Is there more than one Savior? Do you even need a Savior?

> "I am the Lord your *God…*and *you shall know no God but Me*; for there is no Savior besides Me."
>
> —Hos. 13:4

> "I, even I am the Lord and *besides Me there is no Savior.*"
>
> —Isa. 43:11

> "A just God and a *Savior,* there is none besides Me. *Look to Me, and be saved* all you ends of the earth! *For I am God and there is no other.*"
>
> —Isa. 45:21-22

"For this is good and acceptable in the sight of *God our Savior*, who desires all men to be saved and come to the knowledge of the truth."

—1 Tim. 2:3

"…because we trust in the *living God who is the Savior* of all men…"

—1 Tim. 4:10

"God our Savior."

—Titus 1:3

"God our Savior."

—Titus 2:10

"God our Savior."

—Titus 3:4

"To God our Savior."

—Jude 1:25

"And my spirit has rejoiced in *God my Savior.*"
—Luke 1:47

When God says something once, we should believe it. When He says something over and over and over, how can we miss it? We need to realize that God is saying there are no excuses to miss this truth. So, God just told us over and over that He is "God the Savior" and He is the only Savior. "*Besides*

Me there is no Savior." God said it—do you believe it?

So why does the Bible repeatedly mention another Savior if God says He is the only Savior, and there are no other Saviors? God is again saying to us, no excuses, don't miss this. I am going to say this over and over and over. There is only one Savior and you shall call His name................................ JESUS.

"You shall call His name *Jesus, for He shall save* His people from their sins."

—Matt. 1:21

"For there is born to you this day in the city of David a *Savior, who is Christ the Lord.*"

—Luke 2:11

"For we ourselves have heard Him and we know that this is indeed *the Christ, the Savior of the world.*"

—John 4:42

"...through the knowledge of the *Lord and Savior Jesus Christ....*"

—2 Pet. 2:20

"But grow in the grace and knowledge of our *Lord and Savior Jesus Christ.* To Him be glory both now and forever."

—2 Pet. 3:18

"This is a faithful saying and worthy of all acceptance, that *Christ Jesus came into the world to save sinners.*"

—1 Tim. 1:15

"...through Jesus Christ our Savior."

—Titus 3:6

"...the Lord Jesus Christ our Savior."

—Titus 1:4

"But has now been revealed by the appearing of our *Savior Jesus Christ...*"

—2 Tim. 1:10

"...that by the name of *Jesus Christ...* (v.12) *nor is there salvation in any other,* for *there is no other name* under heaven given among men by which we must be saved."

—Acts 4:10 & 12

Jesus is the only one that must save us! Not *might* be save or *should* save. MUST BE SAVE!

Both God and Jesus are proclaimed to be the one and only Savior, yet the Bible repeatedly says there is only one Savior and there cannot be two. Do you see a problem here? If Jesus is God, the one and only Savior is not a problem. If there are two Saviors, are we to choose one over the other? No! There is one God, He alone is the Savior—known to us as Jesus!

Peter uses God and Jesus in the same sentence as the one and only Savior. Why? He knew Jesus was God!

> "...by the righteousness of our *God* and *Savior Jesus Christ.*"
>
> —2 Pet. 1:1

Paul also refers to God and Jesus in the same sentence. He also proclaimed Jesus is God.

> ...looking for the blessed hope and glorious *appearing* of our great *God* and *Savior Jesus Christ.*
>
> —Titus 2:13

If you reject Jesus as your personal Savior, you are rejecting God! If you reject that Jesus is God, you have the wrong Jesus! If you reject Jesus as your Savior, you will miss eternal life. This is not a "straddle the fence" maybe He is, maybe He isn't, statement. It is the difference between eternal life and eternal death.

We Christians are attacked and accused of this biblical truth, possibly as much as anything in our doctrine. We need to share, in love and compassion, that there is only one way. Jesus is the answer! Eternal life is a free gift from God—the one and only God of the Bible! Is that narrow-minded? Yes! But, do consider the source. God makes the rules. We are to trust and obey!

For our citizenship is in heaven, from which we also eagerly wait for *the Savior, the Lord Jesus Christ.*

—Phil. 3:20

Chapter Five

Worship Whom?

If you worship the God of the Bible, whom do you worship?

The Ten Commandments start out by saying:

> "You shall have no other gods before Me. You shall not make for yourself a carved image—any likeness of anything that is in heaven above, or that is in the earth beneath, or that is in the water under the earth; you shall not bow down to them nor serve them. *For I, the Lord your God, am a jealous God.*"
>
> —Exod. 20:3-5

God is not leaving room for any type of god in any situation or location. We are not to honor or serve any god (real or imagined) but the God of the

Bible! And that is stated throughout the Bible. God says He is a "jealous God" many times in the Bible. A strong statement that means God is protective of His sovereign authority. He demands exclusive loyalty from humans and angels.

> Thus says *God the Lord...I am the Lord, that is My name; and My glory I will not give to another.*
> —Isa. 42:5 & 8

> Do not go after other gods to serve them and worship them.
> —Jer. 25:6

> Exalt the Lord our God, and worship at His holy hill; for the Lord our God is holy.
> —Ps. 99:9

> ...For it is written, you shall *worship* the Lord your *God*, and *Him only* you shall serve.
> —Luke 4:8

The Bible tells us to worship God throughout the Old and New Testaments. The Bible tells us to worship the Father and in fact the Father is actively seeking our worship.

> ...*worship the Father*...but the hour is coming, and now is when the *true worshipers will worship the Father* in spirit and truth for *the Father is seeking such to worship Him.*
> —John 4:21 & 23

Worship God only. If you worship the Father are you worshiping God? Yes, most believers do not have a problem with that, but the Bible says to worship Jesus also, and Jesus has no problem accepting worship! So do we worship Jesus in a different way than we worship God?

> (Jesus speaking) "Do you believe in the Son of God?" He (the blind man Jesus healed) answered and said "who is He, Lord, that I may believe in Him?" And Jesus said to him, "you have both seen Him and it is He who is talking to you." Then he said, "Lord, I believe!" And he *worshiped Him.*
>
> —John 9:35-38

This healed man could have said "God in heaven, thank you; I worship you." But he worshiped Jesus and Jesus accepted the worship of the blind man He had just healed. All of this took place in front of many people, some of whom did not like Jesus, but they could not deny the healing of the blind man.

Most people know the story of "the three wise men" who followed the bright star to find Jesus in Bethlehem, at the time of His birth, but why did they want to find Him? Yes, they came bearing gifts, but the real purpose was to worship Jesus.

> ...for we (the wise men) have seen His star in the east and have come to *worship Him* (Jesus)...And when they had come into the house, they saw the

young Child with Mary, His mother, and they *fell
down and worshiped Him.*

—Matt. 2:2 & 11

How about the disciples of Jesus? Did they worship Him? The next two Scriptures are examples
of worship, not to be confused with greeting Him
with a hug.

Jesus met them, saying, "rejoice!" So they came
and held Him by the feet and *worshiped Him.*

—Matt. 28:9

When they saw Him, they worshiped Him; but
some doubted.

—Matt. 28:17

Doubted what? Some doubted that He should be
worshiped. Not to be confused with greeting Him
as one man greets another.

Then Jesus healed a leper and a blind man.

And behold, a leper came and *worshiped Him*,
saying, "Lord, if You are willing, You can make
me clean." Then Jesus put out His hand and
touched him, saying "I am willing; be cleansed."
Immediately his leprosy was cleansed.

—Matt. 8:2-3

Then he (the blind man) said, "Lord, I believe!"
And he worshiped Him (Jesus).

—John 9:38

Jesus not only healed the men, but accepted their worship. If the men were wrong to worship Jesus, Jesus should not have healed them. If Jesus was not to accept worship He should have reprimanded them immediately, as did an angel when John tried to worship him.

> Now I, John, saw and heard these things. And when I heard and saw, *I fell down to worship before the feet of the angel* who showed me these things. Then he said to me, "see that you do not do that. For I am your fellow servant, and of your brethren the prophets, and of those who keep the words of this book. Worship God."
>
> —Rev. 22:8-9

John was totally amazed by a very powerful, intelligent, and glorious-in-appearance, angel (you and I would probably be on our knees too!). John wanted to show great respect and honor to him by bowing at his feet. This angel stopped John immediately and told him to worship God only.

Another example is Cornelius. He tried to worship Peter, and Peter stopped him immediately. Why? So that we humans understand that only God is to be worshiped!

> As Peter was coming in, Cornelius met him and fell down at his feet and worshiped him. But Peter lifted him up, saying "stand up; I myself am also a man."
>
> —Acts 10:25-26

Yet Jesus, being a man, dressed and looking similar to Peter, was worshiped many times and never stopped or corrected anyone. Why did the angel and Peter stop anyone from worshipping them, yet Jesus did not? Because only God is to be worshiped. Jesus is God in the flesh and is to be worshiped.

> "*Look to Me, and be saved*, all you ends of the earth! For *I am God and there is no other*. I have sworn by Myself; the word has gone out of My mouth in righteousness, and shall not return, *that to Me every knee shall bow, every tongue shall take an oath.*"
>
> —Isa. 45:22-23

> ...that at the *name of Jesus every knee should bow*, of those in heaven, and those on the earth, and those under the earth, and that *every tongue should confess that Jesus is Lord*...
>
> —Phil. 2:10-11

These last two Scriptures are almost identical except that one is talking about God and one is talking about Jesus. Every knee will bow to God! Every knee will bow to Jesus! Every tongue will confess to God! Every tongue will confess to Jesus! If Jesus is not God, there is some explaining to do here.

Jesus makes this very clear when speaking to Satan. Jesus knew that only God was to be worshiped. So when He accepts worship it is because He is nothing less than fully God.

(Jesus speaking) "Get behind Me Satan! For it is written, you shall worship the Lord your God, and Him only you shall serve."

—Luke 4:8

Interesting note, Jesus commanded Satan to get behind Him! It was not a request. Only God has the power to command Satan!

Every time someone came to Jesus and worshiped Him, Jesus accepted the worship. Why? Because He is God! Jesus is making a personal statement that He is God.

If Jesus was less than God, why did He not tell people who fell at His feet to stand up and worship God only? He could have said, "Don't worship Me, I am only a man," or, "Don't worship Me, I am an angel," as did other men and even angels. Why? Because Jesus, even though taking on human form, is God.

The Bible tells us that there is one God. Yet we see over and over, the Father, the Son, and the Holy Spirit are always together as One. Many times they are in the same sentence and they always agree, support, and praise each other. The Bible is proclaiming to us that the Father is God, the Son is God, and the Holy Spirit is God.

The main purpose of this book is to focus on Jesus because many professing Christians accept that the Father is God, and since God is spirit, the Holy Spirit is accepted as God. Jesus however, being a man, even though He did many great miracles

41

and spoke with great authority and wisdom, was after all, a man. He could bleed real blood, suffer pain, and die just like every other person that will ever live on this earth. So, how could Jesus be a man and be the one and only Savior and God of all creation? OK, I agree, it is a mystery, but with God all things are possible because the Bible tells us so. To me, the mystery is not how God could become a man, but rather why would He choose to become a man and then suffer and die for us. Wouldn't it be easier just to start over with the human race? Well, God is a God of love, yet He demands perfection. He wants all of His creation spotless and sinless. That means humans and angels must be perfect to be in His presence. And He wants all of creation to have the choice to choose to love and worship Him. Humans, by choice, chose to go against God. God loves us, but had to deal with our sin and rebellion. His perfection demands justice. The penalty for sin is death. If we pay for our own sin, we die (eternal separation from God). Jesus, who is God, is perfect and lived a sinless human life. He chose to die and pay the price for our sin, for all the sins of every human on this earth. His only requirement of us to be forgiven of every sin we have (or will in the future) committed, is to believe that He is God. He has the power and authority to forgive us and make us perfect if we will just ask Him. In return we will start to understand the love of God. We will worship Him and live and love and enjoy God's plan for our lives, throughout eternity, to the fullest, far beyond what we can imagine or dream.

But when He (God) again brings the firstborn (Jesus) into the world, He says: *"Let all the angels of God worship Him."*

—Heb. 1:6

What does *"ALL* the angels" mean? Not only are all the angles in heaven told to worship Jesus, but even the fallen angels (demons) that followed Satan will bow to Jesus.

Then He called His twelve disciples together and gave them power over *all* the demons...

—Luke 9:1

Then the seventy returned with joy, saying "Lord, even the demons are subject to us *in Your name."*

—Luke 10:17

And every creature (angels are created creatures) which is in heaven and on the earth and under the earth and as such as are in the sea, and *all that are in them*, I heard saying: "blessing and honor and glory and power be to Him who sits on the throne, and to the Lamb, forever and ever!"

—Rev. 5:13

...that at the name of **Jesus** *every knee* should bow, of those in heaven, and of those on the earth, and of those under the earth.

—Phil. 2:10

Why do all the angels worship Jesus? Because Jesus is God, and God is a jealous God and will not share his glory with another. God tells us there are no other gods yet He says in...

> But to the Son (Jesus) He (the Father) says: "Your throne, O God, is for ever and ever."
>
> —Heb. 1:8

> All those who go down to the dust shall bow before Him.
>
> —Ps. 22:295

Interesting note #1: After a person dies, it takes a long time (unless cremated) to become dust. Yet, after a persons body turns to dust, every person (saved or lost) will still acknowledge and bow before Jesus. Wow!

Interesting note #2: The definition of the word "worship" in a godly sense means: showing reverence for Deity. The original biblical languages use the same words meaning "worship" whether used in reference to God, or the Father, or Jesus. Some people of our time twist those interpretations so that the exact words that say: "worship God" they gladly interpret to mean worship God. However, when the exact same words say "worship Jesus" they interpret worship in a lesser capacity. Examples would be to respect or honor or give credit to, Jesus. That however, does not mean "worship Jesus" the same as you worship God. Well, the words are exactly the same in the original Greek language, so...be careful! You can give respect, credit, and honor to any person without worshiping them. Jesus is to worshiped. If you do not worship Jesus, your Jesus is *not* the Jesus of the Bible!

Chapter Six

Who Raised Jesus from the Dead?

This Jesus God has raised up.

—Acts 2:32

Let it be known to you all, and to all the people of Israel, that by the name of Jesus Christ of Nazareth, whom you crucified, whom God raised from the dead...

—Acts 4:10

that if you confess with your mouth the Lord Jesus and believe in your heart that God has raised Him from the dead, you will be saved.

—Rom. 10:9

And God both raised up the Lord and will also raise us up by His power.

—1 Cor. 6:14

One of the main beliefs of Christianity is that God has the power to raise the dead. He raised Jesus from the dead three days after He was killed on the cross. One day He will raise every person that has ever lived. Many times the Bible refers to the dead being raised.

But Jesus raised the dead also and Jesus even claimed He raised Himself from the dead.

...I (Jesus) lay down My life that I may take it again. No one takes it from Me, but I lay it down of Myself. I have power to lay it down, and I have power to take it again.

—John 10:17-18

That seems to be a pretty straightforward statement claiming the power of life over death. Jesus of course, does not want us to miss this truth so He states it several times just to make sure there is no doubt as to what He can and will do.

...What sign do You show to us, since You do these things? Jesus answered and said to them, "Destroy this temple, and in three days I will raise it up." Then the Jews said, "It has taken forty-six years to build this temple, and will You raise it up in three days?" But He was speaking of the temple of His body. Therefore, when He had risen from the dead, His disciples remembered that He had said this to them; and they believed the scripture and the word which Jesus had said.

—John 2:18-22

The disciples understood that Jesus was telling them that He would raise His body (temple) in three days and the Bible makes it very clear to us that Jesus' body (and our body) is a temple. For we read in ...

Or do you not know that your body is the temple of the Holy Spirit who is in you...?

—I Cor. 6:19

Do you not know that you are the temple of God...?

—I Cor. 3:16

For you are the temple of the living God.

—2 Cor. 6:16

The Father also proclaims He raised Jesus from the dead.

... that just as Christ was raised from the dead by the glory of the Father...

—Rom. 6:4

Paul, an apostle (not from men nor through man, but through Jesus Christ and God the Father who raised Him from the dead).

—Gal. 1:1

The Holy Spirit also raised Jesus from the dead.

But if the Spirit of Him who raised Jesus from the dead dwells in you, He who raised Christ from the dead will also give life to your mortal bodies through His Spirit who dwells in you.

—Rom. 8:11

It is the Spirit who gives life.

— John 6:63

For Christ also suffered once for sins, the just for the unjust, that He might bring us to God, being put to death in the flesh but made alive by the Spirit.

—1 Pet. 3:18

Jesus says he raised Himself from the dead. The Father and the Holy Spirit say they raised Jesus from the dead. Yet, over and over God claims to raise the dead. And there is ONLY ONE GOD! So...

Why should it be thought incredible by you that God raises the dead?

— Acts 26:8

How about the Father and the Son (Jesus) in the same sentence stating the power to raise the dead.

> "For as the Father raises the dead and gives life to them, even so the Son gives life to whom He will... that all should honor the Son just as they honor the Father. He who does not honor the Son does not honor the Father who sent Him.
>
> — John 5:21 & 23

If we believe that the Father is God, then we are also to believe that Jesus is God. For we are told to honor Jesus just the same as we honor the Father. And how do we honor the Father? We worship Him! If we do not worship Jesus as we worship the Father, we do not worship God!

So, Jesus not only raised Himself from the dead, but as we read in the last Scripture, Jesus has the power to "give life to whom He will." Jesus will raise all the dead when we reach the end of time as we now know it. For some a celebration (HIGHLY recommended)! For some a day of judgment (NOT recommended)!

> "And this is the will of Him who sent Me, that everyone who sees the Son and believes in Him may have everlasting life; and I will raise him up the last day."
>
> —John 6:40

To show the power He had over death, Jesus also raised many individual people from the dead that had only been dead a short time.

> Then He (Jesus) came and touched the open coffin, and those who carried him stood still. And He said, "Young man, I say to you, arise." So he who was dead sat up and began to speak.
> —Luke 7:14-15

When Jesus brought this man back to life, many of his disciples and a large crowd were following Him to the city of Nain. Plus, as the dead man was being carried out of this city, a large funeral crowd was there as well. I don't know how many people it takes to make two large crowds, but I am sure there were enough witnesses there so that this miracle could not be denied.

> And they ridiculed Him (Jesus), knowing that she was dead. But He put them all outside, took her by the hand and called, saying, "Little girl, arise." Then her spirit returned, and she arose immediately.
> —Luke 8:53-55

> Now when He (Jesus) had said these things, He cried with a loud voice, "Lazarus, come forth!" And he who had died came out bound hand and foot with grave clothes, and his face was wrapped

with a cloth. Jesus said to them, "Loose him, and let him go."

— John 11:43-44

Jesus healed the sick and raised the dead every place He went. I haven't found any evidence that anyone stayed sick or died in the presence of Jesus in the New Testament, except at the cross. I am not saying people were not sick or dying in His presence, I just don't know of an example to the contrary. Jesus is about life, abundant and eternal!

Even the people who were against Him could not argue His power over death. Instead, some would criticize Him for the miracles He did, because He did them on the Sabbath or performed them on people who were openly sinners. Many times He raised the dead and healed the sick in public places and people would follow Him, just to watch Him perform miracles. A free show, no cover charge! And the end result; eternal life, if they would believe in the saving grace of Jesus!

I would like to quote another Scripture on the miracles of Jesus.

And there are also many other things that Jesus did, which if they were written one by one, I suppose that even the world itself could not contain the books that would be written. Amen.

—John 21:25

This is a fascinating Scripture. A person could easily read it without giving it much thought. I'm not going to try to interpret it verbatim, but rather just add a few comments. We know that Jesus miraculously provided food for thousands of people several times. He knew the future; what people were thinking; what they were about to speak; He cast out demons; walked on water; changed water to wine; calmed the winds and waves of the sea. He healed lepers, paralysis, hemorrhaging, the blind, the mute, a withered hand, epilepsy, dropsy; suddenly appeared in a room even though the windows and doors were shut, and restored an ear that had been cut off.

The last Scripture quote says Jesus did many other things. I think that means many other things than what we already know Jesus did. When John said "I suppose that even the world itself could not contain the books that would be written." He may have meant that statement to be a whisper of humor, or a statement as to how well he knew Jesus, or even a rhetorical challenge, yet for the sake of argument, if you were there and tried to keep count of every miracle of Jesus, John was saying, bring extra pencils and all the paper you and your donkey can carry, because you are going to need it!

Just one more reference on miracles. It is a future miracle far beyond our comprehension but, trust God, it will come to pass! What is it? Well! Why not look it up in your own Bible? (Rev. 21:1-27).

Chapter Seven

Jesus and God, Who Can Tell the Difference?

Most of these Scriptures need little explanation. By reading them one after the other you can see that the message is very clear: Jesus is God!

> ...Christ the *power of God* and the *wisdom of God.*
>
> —1 Cor. 1:24

> ...the glory of *Christ, who is the image of God...*
> —2 Cor. 4:4

> Therefore the Jews sought all the more to kill Him (Jesus), because He not only broke the Sabbath, but also said that God was His Father, *making Himself equal with God.*
>
> —John 5:18

Why did some of the Jews want to kill Jesus? Because Jesus said He was equal with God. The next Scripture reinforces why some Jews wanted to kill Jesus.

> "I and My Father are one." Then the Jews took up stones again to stone Him. Jesus answered them, "many good works I have shown you from My Father. For which of those works do you stone Me?" The Jews answered Him, saying, "For a good work we do not stone You, but for blasphemy, and *because You, being a Man, make Yourself God.*"
>
> —John 10:30-33

When Jesus said, "I and My Father are one," He did not just mean one in purpose. The Jews knew Jesus was claiming to be equal with the Father and that would make Him God. The Jews thought they were one in purpose with God by trying to kill a Man who said He was God.

> And after eight days His disciples were again inside, and Thomas with them. Jesus came, the doors being shut (walked through the wall I assume) and stood in the midst, and said, "Peace to you!" Then He said to Thomas, "Reach your finger here, and look at My hands; and reach your hand here, and put it into My side. Do not be unbelieving, but believing." And Thomas answered and said to Him, "*My Lord and my God!*" Jesus

said to him, "Thomas, because you have seen Me,
you have believed. *Blessed* are those who have
not seen and yet have believed."

—John 20:26-29

Blessed are those who have not seen what? That
Jesus did rise from the dead and that He is God (as
Thomas said to Jesus "My Lord and my God"). "Who
have not seen" means us! That is a blessing for you
and me, if we believe.

And they stoned Stephen as he was *calling on God
and saying, Lord Jesus,* receive my spirit."

—Acts 7:59

Stephen sure believed that Jesus was God. He
could have said "God" or "Lord" receive my spirit
and been correct, but he understood that Jesus was
God and called Him by name.

And we know that the Son of God has come
and has given us an understanding, that we may
know Him who is true, in His son *Jesus Christ.
This is the true God and eternal life.*

—1 John 5:20

Who does that last verse say is the true God? I
do believe it says "Jesus Christ" is the true God and
eternal life!

God was manifested *in the flesh.*

—1 Tim. 3:16

Webster's dictionary defines "manifest" as: obvious; to make clear or evident; reveal; to prove. So, to exchange any of those definitions in the place of "manifested" it does indeed place God in human form, which has to be Jesus.

God was *obviously* in the flesh.

God was *made clear* in the flesh.

God was *evidently* in the flesh.

God was *revealed* in the flesh.

God was *proved* in the flesh.

Thank you Webster's dictionary for your input!

> Let this mind be in you which was also in *Christ Jesus, who being in the form of God did not consider it robbery to be equal with God.*
>
> —Phil. 2:5-6

If Jesus is equal with God and there is only one God, then Jesus is God and took on human flesh. Or we could say God is Jesus and took on human flesh.

> For in Him (Jesus) dwells *all the fullness of the Godhead bodily.*
>
> —Col. 2:9

Wow! All (all means *all!*) the fullness (fullness means everything that is God) dwells in Jesus.

The gospel of John starts out declaring that Jesus is indeed God in the flesh.

> In the beginning was the *Word*, and the *Word* was with God and *the Word was God*. All things were made through Him, and without Him nothing was made that was made.
>
> —John 1:1-2

So, *God is the Word* and He created everything that exists. The Bible also tells us that Jesus is the *Word*, which means that Jesus created all things and is God in the flesh. Jesus had to have existed before the creation of the world or He could not have created it.

> He (Jesus) was in the world, and the *world was made through Him*, and the world did not know Him.
>
> —John 1:10

> And the *Word became flesh and dwelt among us*.
>
> —John 1:14

God is the Word and the Word became flesh. How do we explain God becoming flesh? Unless we are talking about Jesus, that will be difficult. What is important here is to notice that God is the Word, not that He became the Word. God has always been the Word. God has not always been flesh though. God did become flesh so that He could physically face-to-face let humans better relate to Him. And of course because He was perfect, He could shed His perfect blood to pay the price for our transgression against His law.

Since "the Word was God," every time the "Word" is used, we could say "God" instead of Word. Another way to read these verses could be: "In the beginning was God, and God was with God, and God was God...and God became flesh and dwelt among us.

The *Word becoming flesh* is referring to Jesus in particular, though. Two references:

> ...and His (Jesus) name is called the *Word of God.*
>
> —Rev. 19:13

I'm sure you have heard in prayers and/or read in books and/or sung songs that use the phrase, "the Father, Son, and Holy Spirit." In one case the Bible leaves out the Son (Jesus) and includes "the Word" where Jesus (the Son) would be.

> For there are three that bear witness in heaven: the Father, the Word, and the Holy Spirit; and these three are one.
>
> —1 John 5:7

The Father is God, the Word (obviously referring to Jesus) is God, and the Holy Spirit is God. These three are the one true God!

Since Jesus is the Word, one more way we could read in John chapter one would be: "In the beginning was Jesus, and Jesus was with God, and Jesus was God...and Jesus became flesh and dwelt among us. God in the flesh!

...But Jesus sent him away, saying "Return to your own house, and tell *what great things God* has done for you." And he went his way and proclaimed throughout the whole city *what great things Jesus* had done for him.

—Luke 8:38-39

This man was told to proclaim God and yet he proclaimed Jesus. Why? Truly he believed that Jesus was God!

He (Jesus) is the *image of the invisible God*...For by Him (Jesus) all things were created that are in heaven and that are on the earth, visible and invisible, whether thrones or dominions or principalities or powers. All things were created through Him and for Him. And He is before all things, and in Him all things consist.

—Col. 1:15-16

Want to see the invisible God? Look at Jesus! Jesus created all things and He holds all things (not some or most, but *all* things) together.

Jesus possess all the wisdom and power of God.

...to the knowledge of the mystery of God, both of the Father and of Christ, in whom are hidden all the treasures of wisdom and knowledge.

—Col. 2:2-3

Everything God created was created by Jesus. All the wisdom God has, Jesus has. Why? Because Jesus is God!

I am obviously focusing on Jesus in this book. However I must state this now and I will again—the Father and the Holy Spirit are co-equal with Jesus. These three are the one true God! Christianity refers to this as the Trinity. Do I understand the Trinity? NO! Can I explain the Trinity? Not very well! Does the Bible proclaim the Trinity? Yes! Do I believe in the Trinity? Absolutely! Do *you* believe in the Trinity? Is the word Trinity in the Bible? No, but neither is Sunday school, Sabbath school (Even though the word "school" is mentioned in Acts 19:9) or theocratic kingdom, however these concepts are taught throughout God's Word. Even the word Bible is not in the Bible, yet it is the most published book of all time. That God is a Triune God is taught throughout the Old and New Testaments is not only of great importance, it is a salvation issue. If you are trusting in a Jesus that is a man, an ascended being, or an angel, you have the wrong Jesus. If you do accept that Jesus is God, celebrate the truth that is within you, for your knowledge and understanding has been greatly increased. Share with others the hope that is within you!

Chapter Eight

Who Should Get All the Glory?

Well, God says:

Thus says *God* the Lord...I am the Lord, that is My name; and *My glory I will not give to another.*

—Isa. 42:5 & 8

And *I will not give My glory to another.*

—Isa. 48:11

Now to our God and Father be *glory for ever and ever.*

—Phil. 4:20

...according to the will of our God and Father, *to whom be glory forever and ever.* Amen.

—Gal. 1:4-5

...to *God* who *alone* is wise, be honor and *glory for ever and ever.* Amen.

—1 Tim. 1:17

To God our Savior, who alone is wise, *be glory* and majesty, dominion and power, both *now and forever*, Amen.

—Jude 1:25

Oh, the depth of His riches both of the wisdom and the knowledge of *God*...For of Him are all things, to whom be *glory forever.* Amen.

—Rom. 11:33 & 36

But may the God of all grace, who called us to His eternal glory...

—1 Pet. 5:10

It is pretty obvious that God's glory is forever and ever and He is not willing to share that glory with anyone else! The Father's glory is mentioned in two passages above and then this one, The Lord's prayer:

Our Father in heaven...for Yours is the kingdom and the power and the glory forever. Amen.

—Matt. 6:9 & 13

And then wouldn't you know it, the Bible says Jesus has glory forever. The same *glory forever* that God is not willing to share with anyone else.

...working in you what is well pleasing in His sight, through *Jesus Christ, to whom be glory forever and ever.* Amen.

—Heb. 13:21

but grow in the grace and knowledge of our Lord and Savior *Jesus Christ. To Him be the glory both now and forever.* Amen

—2 Pet. 3:18

My brethren, do not hold the faith of our Lord Jesus Christ, *the Lord of glory,* with partiality.

—James 2:1

Which none of the rulers of this age knew; for had they known, they would not have crucified the *Lord of glory.* (Jesus was the Lord of glory that was crucified).

—1 Cor. 2:8

If the Bible says that God will not give His glory to anyone else, why does the Bible also say Jesus is to get all the glory too? Again, can I explain the Trinity? Not very well! Can I show biblical proof of the Trinity? Yes! If you believe the Bible, Jesus can be nothing less than God!

Chapter Nine

Who Is
the Shepherd?

The Lord is my Shepherd.

—Ps. 23:1

Behold, the *Lord God* shall come with a strong hand, And His arm shall rule for Him; Behold His reward is with Him, and His work before Him. He will feed His flock like a *shepherd*;

—Isa. 40:10-11

He (God) who scattered Israel will gather him, and keep him as a *shepherd* does his flock.

—Jer. 31:10

For thus says the *Lord God*: Indeed *I Myself* will search for My sheep and seek them out, *as a shepherd* seeks out his flock.

—Ezek. 34:11

And as for you O My flock, thus says the Lord
God: "Behold, I shall judge between sheep and
sheep, between rams and goats."

—Ezek. 34:17

"You are My flock, the flock of My pasture; *you
are men*, and I am your God," says the Lord
God.

—Ezek. 34:31

God is not talking about sheep that are animals
but rather "<u>You are My flock; you are men</u>." God
is the Shepherd of men! Also notice that God will
judge the sheep and the goats. In the next verse we
notice Jesus is the Shepherd and He will divide the
same sheep from the goats.

"When the Son of Man (Jesus) comes in His glory,
and all the holy angels with Him, then He will sit
on the throne of His glory. All the nations will be
gathered before Him, and He will separate them
one from another, as a *shepherd* divides his sheep
from the goats."

—Matt. 25:31-32

For you were like sheep going astray, but have
now returned to the Shepherd (Jesus) and Over-
seer of your souls.

—1 Pet. 2:25

and when the <u>Chief Shepherd (Jesus)</u> appears, you will receive the crown of glory that does not fade away.

—1 Pet. 5:4

Then Jesus said to them again, "Most assuredly, I say to you, I am the door of the sheep…<u>I am the good shepherd</u>. The good shepherd gives His life for the sheep…I am the good shepherd; and I know My sheep…and there will be *one flock and one shepherd*…My sheep hear My voice, and I know them, and they follow Me. They shall never perish.

—John 10:7 & 11 & 14 & 16 & 27-28

God is the shepherd and He has a reward for His followers. Jesus is the shepherd and He gives His life for His followers. The followers of Jesus will be given the crown of glory and they will never perish, yet there is only *one flock and one Shepherd*. There is only one Chief Shepherd, and we call him Jesus!

Chapter Ten

Am I Who I Am?
(Part One)

The words "I AM" is a self proclaimed title used by God. Some of the "I AM'S" in the Bible indicate and/or proclaim His self-existence. Some of the "I AM'S" are stating "of a truth" or "listen to Me" or "look to Me" or "don't miss this." "I *AM" is also stating there is no other like Me.* "I AM" precedes God, the Lord, and Jesus over two hundred times in the Bible. We are going to look at just a few of these Scriptures so that we understand when God says He is the "I AM," He is stating that He is the one and only true God. There is no one like Him. There never has been a time that He did not exist, and there will never be a time that He will cease to exist. So God's claim to us is: I AM the Self-Existent One! I AM eternal!

And *God* said to Moses, "*I AM WHO I AM.*" And He said, "Thus you shall say to the children of Israel, '*I AM* has sent me to you.'" Moreover God said to Moses, "Thus you shall say to the children of Israel: 'The Lord God of your fathers, the God of Abraham, the God of Isaac, and the God of Jacob, has sent me to you. This is *My name forever*, and this is My memorial to *all generations*.
— Exod. 3:14-15

If "I AM" is God's name forever and a name to all generations, He sure as Heaven is not going to share that name (title) with anyone else. Just to make sure we understand this truth, God repeats Himself several times.

...*I AM Almighty God*; walk before Me...
— Gen. 17:1

Also God said to him: "*I AM God Almighty*...
— Gen. 35:11

And they shall know that *I AM* the Lord their God...
— Exod. 29:46

I AM God, your God!
— Ps. 50:7

Be still and know that *I AM* God.
— Ps. 46:10

I AM the Lord, that is *My name…*

—Isa. 42:8

Says the Lord, "that *I AM* God. Indeed before the day was, *I AM* He…

—Isa. 43:12-13

God is not shy about saying "I AM" is His name and that "I AM" existed before the world was created.

I AM the Lord, and *there is no other.*

—Isa. 45:5

For thus says the Lord, Who created the heavens, Who is God, Who formed the earth and made it, Who has established it, Who did not create it in vain, Who formed it to be inhabited: *I AM* the Lord, and *there is no other.*

—Isa. 45:18

Behold, *I AM* the Lord, the *God of all flesh.* Is there anything too hard for Me?

—Jer. 32:27

God is not trying to prove anything by saying "I AM." He is stating the fact that He does exist, He has always existed and that He always will exist. He created all things and He created all life. He also has the power to do anything He pleases. Nothing is too hard for God.

Jesus claimed to be the eternal "I AM" as well, proclaiming that He is God. Let's take a look and see if it isn't so.

> "Your father Abraham rejoiced to see My day, and he saw it and was glad." Then the Jews said to Him, "you are not yet fifty years old, and you have seen Abraham?" *Jesus* said to them, "most assuredly, I say to you, before Abraham was, *I AM*." Then they took up stones to throw at Him...
>
> —John 8:56-59

The reason the Jews wanted to stone Jesus was that He said that He knew Abraham and Abraham knew Him. The Jews were very aware that Abraham was born several thousand years before Jesus was born. And then Jesus said to these Jews that He was the "I AM," meaning that He was the Self-Existent One, God Almighty! Jesus was either a liar, insane, or God. He gave the Jews (and us) no other choice as to what to believe. Just as God referred to himself as "I AM" over and over, so did Jesus over and over.

> And Jesus came and spoke to them, saying..."*I AM with you always*, even to the end of the age."
>
> —Matt. 28:18 & 20

How could Jesus be with everyone till the end of this age unless He is God? Only God can be everywhere at the same time. Actually that Scripture should also be interpreted that not only is Jesus with us now, but He is also at the end of time waiting for us, because He already knows everything that will happen.

> ...*for I AM with you*; be not dismayed, *for I AM your God.*
>
> —Isa. 41:10

Since "I AM" is a definition or title of God, as you read through these next few verses you will notice they are all about Jesus, yet you will see God in the center of these Scriptures.

> (Jesus speaking) "For where two or three are gathered in My name, *I AM* there in the midst of them."
>
> —Matt. 18:20

This can only mean that Jesus is everywhere at the same time. Christian churches, Bible studies, prayer groups; yes, even several people playing Christian bingo; any time day or night, Jesus is there!

> (Jesus speaking) Yet *I AM* among you as the One who serves.
>
> —Luke 22:27

And *Jesus* said to them, "*I AM* the bread of life"…"*I AM* the bread which came down from heaven." "*I AM* the living bread…"

—John 6:35 & 41 & 51

Then *Jesus* spoke to them again, saying "*I AM* the light of the world (1 JOHN 1:5 says "God is light")…"*I AM* One who bears witness of Myself…" "*I AM* from above…" "*I AM* He…" "then you will know that *I AM* He…"

—John 8:12 & 18 & 23 & 24 & 28

(Jesus) "As long as *I AM* in the world, *I AM* the light of the world."

—John 9:5

(Jesus) "*I AM* the door. If anyone enters by Me, he will be saved." "*I AM* the good shepherd." (PSALM 23:1 The Lord is my Shepherd.)

—John 10:9 & 11

Jesus said to her, "*I AM* the resurrection and the life."

—John 11:25

(Jesus) "If anyone serves Me, let him follow Me; and where *I AM*, there My servant will be also."

—John 12:26

(Jesus) "You call Me teacher and Lord, and you say well, for so <u>AM I</u>."

—John 13:13

(Jesus) "Now I tell you before it comes, that when it does come to pass, *you may believe that I AM He*."

—John 13:19

(Jesus) "Where *I AM* going you cannot follow Me now, but you shall follow Me afterward."

—John 13:36

(Jesus) "And if I go to prepare a place for you, I will come again and receive you to Myself; that where *I AM*, there you may be also."

—John 14:3

Jesus said to him, *I AM* the way, the truth, and the life."

—John 14:6

(Jesus) "*I AM* the true vine."

—John 15:1

God tells us that "I AM" is His name and He won't share that name with anyone, yet Jesus does not seem to hold back when He states that He is "I AM."

In these next few verses I almost find a touch of humor, if it were not so sad. The Jews (and soldiers) were in the presence of Holy God and were so blind and stubborn, they could not see it. When Jesus says to them "I AM" they *all fell to the ground*. Nobody can take Jesus as a prisoner, He freely went with them knowing that He was allowing Himself to be arrested and killed for the sins of the world.

> Then Judas, having received a detachment of troops, and officers from the chief priests and Pharisees, came there with lanterns, torches, and weapons. *Jesus* therefore, *knowing all things* that would come upon Him, went forward and said to them "whom are you seeking?" They answered Him, "Jesus of Nazareth." *Jesus said* to them, "*I AM He*," Now when He said to them, "*I AM He*," *they drew back and fell to the ground*. Then He asked them again, "Whom are you seeking?" And they said, "Jesus of Nazareth." *Jesus answered, "I have told you that I AM He."*
>
> —John 18:3-8

A "detachment of troops and officers" could have been as many as six hundred soldiers with weapons. On this occasion maybe less, but they did expect Jesus and his followers to resist arrest and that is why they carried weapons. So it did appear that Jesus and a few followers were outnumbered by an over whelming number (not really though, as Jesus could have called on over 72,000 angels to come to His rescue. One Angel would probably have been sufficient, the way I see it! Matt. 26:53 twelve legions at 6,000 per legion).

As the troops approached Jesus to arrest Him, He just spoke words to them and they *all fell to the ground*! If I were a soldier, after witnessing that, I would not want to have been the first to put a hand on Jesus to bind Him and lead Him away! Jesus wanted them (and us of course) to know the truth. He has the power and the control in every situation, even when being arrested. It was not (is not) the will of Jesus to force anyone to believe. Jesus does remind us though...

> "But whoever denies Me before men, I will also deny before My Father in heaven."
>
> —Matt. 10:33

All people should hear the truth about Jesus, but no one can be forced to believe. According to the Bible, there is only *one way to eternal life* and that way is Jesus. Either you believe that or you do not—it is a choice. It may not seem fair, it may not be how you would like it to be, but Jesus said:

> "*I AM* the way, the truth, and the life. *No one* comes to the Father except through Me."
>
> —John 14:6

That truth is not me talking to you, it is Jesus talking to you. If it offends you, complain to the one who said it. Maybe the offended person could cut that Scripture out of the Bible, but then what would that person do with this one?

> "that by the name of *Jesus*...nor is there *salvation* in any other, for there is *no other name* given among men by which we *must be saved.*"
>
> —Acts 4:10 & 12

I don't see that we are given a choice as to how we obtain eternal life. However, we do have the ability to choose eternal life or eternal death. We can choose to reject the one and only way God has provided for us, but His terms are: salvation through Jesus Christ only! Jesus is the narrow gate, every other path leads to destruction.

> "Enter by the narrow gate; for wide is the gate and broad is the way that leads to destruction, and there are many who go in by it."
>
> —Matt. 7:13

Yes, the gate (Jesus Christ) is narrow, in fact so narrow that, if you miss that gate and try to enter the Eternal Kingdom by any other gate, you will end up in hell by your own choice. So just what is the narrow gate, and is it difficult? Narrow, yes! Difficult, no! Anyone can enter this narrow gate! You don't need legs or eyes or money or education or good looks or a religious tag or good works for humanity. You do need...

> ...If you confess with your mouth the Lord Jesus and believe in you heart that God has raised Him from the dead, *you will be saved.* For with

the heart one believes unto righteousness, and with the mouth confession is made unto salvation. For the Scripture says, "Whoever believes on Him will not be put to shame." For there is no distinction between Jew and Greek, for the same Lord over all is rich to all who call upon Him. For "*whoever calls on the name of the Lord shall be saved.*"

—Rom. 10: 9-13

Sometimes I think my prayer life has been lived similar to this next paragraph. I hope it is not a reflection of your life!

God forgive me for not sharing Your eternal truth as much as I could. I am afraid I might offend someone. I am sure it is better that I not embarrass myself or possibly confuse some people that I come in contact with. I should let them find or believe their own truth. I, myself, believe Your Word only because several people over a period of many years shared Your truth with me and prayed for me; and one day I accepted Jesus Christ, by choice, being led by the Holy Spirit, as my personal Savoir. But if people I know want to be saved, they can read the Bible or start going to church on their own. They don't need to hear Your truth from me. Besides, maybe there is another way…. After all, is God's plan for eternal life really a narrow path or even that important?

Yes, it is important! Yes, it is narrow! Yes, it is eternal!

God forgive me!

Chapter Eleven

Am I Who I Am?
(Part Two)

When we are around people who talk about themselves a lot, we hear over and over: I said this, I did that, I saw this, I told you, I knew, I wasn't fooled, I can do that, I'm the one, I was first, I do know, I like, I love, I will, I will not, I...I...I... I...I.

For the most part, we do not enjoy being around people like that very long. However, God and Jesus use the word "I" (and "I AM") more times than we would want to count (I started to count "I" in the Bible, then realized it would take longer to count the number of times God and Jesus said "I" than it would to write this book, so, I gave up). "I" is just part of this "I AM" chapter. The reason God uses the "I" word so much is that He is the most qualified to explain who He is and what He has done. And all of His claims, promises, and descriptions are 100%

true. So, in the case of the Almighty, I or I AM is an expression of truth and love for us.

We have more "I AM's" to consider now, though our main focus will be studying the statements that follow "I AM." They are: *"First and Last, Alpha and Omega,* and *Beginning and End."* These Scriptures are very powerful in expressing the Deity of Jesus Christ.

> *"I AM the First* and *I AM the Last*; *besides Me there is no God."*
>
> —Isa. 44:6

> "I, the Lord, am the *first*; And with the *last* I AM He."
>
> —Isa. 41:4

> "Listen to Me, O Jacob, and Israel, My called: I AM He, *I AM the First, I AM also the Last."*_
>
> —Isa. 48:12

As we have just read, God is the First and the Last. First and Last is another title and/or identification God has chosen to express Himself. Obviously this next verse has to be describing God as well, because God has established that He is the First and the Last.

> "Do not be afraid; *I AM the First* and the *Last*. I AM He who lives, *and was dead*, and behold, I AM alive forevermore."
>
> —Rev. 1:17-18

If the First and the Last is God, and the First and the Last was dead, when did God die and then become alive for evermore? We know that Jesus died—that is how God could die. Jesus is the "I AM." We know this because Jesus also uses the very same "First and Last" title in:

> "These things says the *First* and the *Last, who was dead*, and came to life."
>
> —Rev. 2:8

Here again, who is speaking? The First and the Last—God—is speaking. Yet *the First and the Last was dead* and then came to life. God died? Then came back to life? The Bible is very specific on this, Yet how could God die? We know Jesus is the one who died. Jesus is the one who rose from the dead. The Bible says Jesus is also the First and the Last! Jesus is God in the form of a man.

There can only be one first. The first to score, the first to cross the finish line, the first get done, etc. Everyone can't be first. There is only one last. If you think you are the last one done, but then someone else gets done after you, you are not last. So when God says He is the first and the last how can Jesus say He is the first and the last? If Jesus is God, this is not a problem.

> I (John) heard behind me a loud voice, as a trumpet, saying, "I AM the Alpha and the Omega, the First and the Last...then I turned to see the voice that spoke with me. And having turned I saw

> seven golden lamp stands, and in the midst of
> the seven lamp stands One like the Son of Man,
> clothed with a garment down to the feet and
> girded about the chest with a golden band...and
> when *I saw Him*, I fell at His feet as dead. But *He
> laid His right hand on me*, saying to me, "Do not
> be afraid; *I AM the First and the Last*."
>
> —Rev. 1:10-13 & 17

At that moment in time, John may not have been
sure who Jesus was, for he says, "One like the son
of Man." John did see the Jesus he knew, but also
saw, (Rev. 1:14 & 15) His hair "white as wool" and
"His eyes like a flame of fire" and "His voice as the
sound of many waters."

We have all seen before and after pictures that
can sometimes catch us off guard. No wonder John
fell at his feet as dead! What is important here is
that John saw and felt the right hand of the one
who says He is the First and Last, which means he
saw and felt the hand of God, then called Him the
son of Man, who of course is Jesus. I counted over
seventy times in the New Testament where *Jesus is
identified as the "Son of Man."* Let's look at just three
passages. Jesus is speaking and identifies Himself as
the Son of Man in each passage.

> "But that you may know that the *Son of Man* has
> power on earth to forgive sins"...then He said to
> the paralytic, "Arise, take up your bed, and go
> to your house."
>
> —Matt. 9:6

"Then the sign of the *Son of Man* will appear in heaven, and then all the tribes of the earth will mourn, and they will see the *Son of Man* coming on the clouds of heaven with power and great glory."

—Matt. 24:30

"Watch therefore, and pray always that you may be counted worthy to escape all these things that will come to pass, and to stand before the *Son of Man*."

—Luke 21:36

The Son of Man has the power and attributes of Jesus. Jesus has the power and attributes of God and there is only one God!

Let's back up to Revelation 1:11. It starts out, "I AM the Alpha and Omega, the First and the Last." Alpha and Omega is synonymous with First and Last, so it is a different way of saying the same thing. It is another title of God, and another title that is also used by Jesus.

"I AM the Alpha and Omega, the Beginning and the End," says the Lord, "who is and who was and who is to come, *the Almighty*."

—Rev. 1:8

This Scripture establishes that Alpha and Omega is Almighty God then adds, "the Beginning and the

End," which is another way of expressing the same title for Almighty God.

> And He said to me "It is done! I AM the Alpha and Omega, the Beginning and the End. I will give of the fountain of the water of life freely to him who thirsts. He who overcomes shall inherit all things, and I will be his God."
>
> —Rev. 21:6-7

Again, God is speaking. He is Alpha and Omega and the Beginning and the End. In the next Scripture we see Alpha and Omega, the Beginning and the End, and the First and Last, all three titles in the same sentence, all titles belonging to God, and yet, take note on who is speaking.

> "I AM the Alpha and Omega, the Beginning and the End, the First and the Last."..."*I, Jesus* have sent My angel to testify to you these things in the churches."
>
> —Rev. 22:13 & 16

Well slam on our spiritual brakes. Can Jesus make all the same claims as God, use all the same names as God, use all the same titles as God, and be anything less than God? Jesus is either insane, a liar, or God Almighty!

"I AM" is one of the shortest complete sentences in the written language, yet God's claim of always existing (past, present, and future) is expressed in truth in that powerful sentence.

"I AM" is one of the shortest complete sentences in the written language, yet *Jesus* is claiming that He has always existed (past, present, and future) and that He is Almighty God!

Chapter Twelve

Is There More Than One Kingdom?

Whether you are a born-again Christian or not, you have probably heard this prayer either read or prayed. Most likely you have repeated this prayer yourself. The study word we are looking for is *kingdom,* and it is stated twice.

> "Our *Father* in heaven, Hallowed be Your name. *Your kingdom* come. Your will be done on earth as it is in heaven. Give us this day our daily bread. And forgive us our debts, as we forgive our debtors. And lead us not into temptation, but deliver us from the evil one. For *Yours is the kingdom* and the power and the glory forever. Amen.
> —Matt. 6:9-13

This prayer (by Jesus) tells us to pray for the Father's kingdom to come to earth. It also tells

91

us that the Father's kingdom and His power and glory will last forever. Yes, The Father does have a kingdom!

> "But I (Jesus) say to you, I will not drink of this fruit of the vine from now on until that day when I drink it new with you in My *Father's kingdom.*
>
> —Matt. 26:29

Jesus was physically eating and drinking with the disciples at this time and He is reassuring the disciples that they will physically meet and eat and drink with Him sometime in the future, in the Father's kingdom. The Father's kingdom is an eternal kingdom and also a physical kingdom because there will be eating and drinking in His kingdom.

In truth! The Father has a kingdom. The Lord also has a kingdom that will never end!

> All Your works shall praise You, *O Lord*, and your saints shall bless You. They shall speak of the glory of *Your kingdom*, and talk of Your power, to make known to the sons of men His mighty acts, And the glorious majesty of *His kingdom. Your kingdom is an everlasting kingdom.*
>
> —Ps. 145:10-13

> Yours, O Lord, is the greatness, the power and the glory, the victory and the majesty; for all that is in heaven and in the earth is Yours; *Yours*

is the kingdom, O Lord, and You are exalted as head over all.

> —1 Chron. 29:11

Yes, the Lord has a kingdom that is everlasting. Next we will read about the kingdom that God has and it is also everlasting.

To all peoples, nations and languages that dwell in all the earth: Peace be multiplied to you. I thought it good to declare the signs and wonders that the *Most High God* has worked for me. How great are His signs, *His kingdom is an everlasting kingdom.*

> —Dan. 4:1-3

"But *seek first the kingdom of God* and His righteousness, and all these things shall be added to you."

> —Matt. 6:33

Now when one of those who sat at the table with Him heard these things, he said to Him, "Blessed is he who shall *eat bread* in *the kingdom of God.*

> —Luke 14:15

That you would walk worthy of *God* who calls you into *His own kingdom* and glory.

> —1 Thess. 2:12

Four points to remember: (1) God has a kingdom that is everlasting. (2) It is His kingdom. (3)

We are to seek *first* God's kingdom. (4) And blessed are the people that will eat bread in the physical kingdom of God.

OK, the Father has a kingdom, the Lord has a kingdom, God has a kingdom—does anyone else have a kingdom that will last forever?

> Then the angel said to her, "Do not be afraid, Mary, for you have found favor with God. And behold, you will conceive in your womb and bring forth a Son, and shall call His name *Jesus.* And He will reign over the house of Jacob forever, *and of His kingdom there will be no end.*"
>
> —Luke 1:30 & 33

Wow! Jesus has a kingdom too! Let's see now, I think that adds up to four kingdoms that will last forever. So, will there be eating and drinking in the kingdom of Jesus?

> (Jesus speaking) "That you may *eat and drink at My table in My kingdom…*"
>
> —Luke 22:30

Yes, there will be eating and drinking in the kingdom of Jesus.

> Then he said to *Jesus,* "Lord, remember me when you come into *your kingdom.*" And Jesus said to him, "Assuredly, I say to you, today you will be with me in Paradise."
>
> —Luke 23:42-43

The thief on the cross was acknowledging to Jesus that he believed Jesus had a kingdom and he wanted to be part of it. Jesus did not deny this eternal kingdom, but rather encouraged this man that he would see Paradise (at least part of the kingdom) before that very day was over.

> For so an entrance will be supplied to you abundantly into the *everlasting kingdom of our Lord and Savior Jesus Christ.*
>
> —2 Pet. 1:11

Who's kingdom? Jesus Christ's! How long will it last? Forever!

OK, time for a review:

1. There will be eating and drinking in the *Father's kingdom.*
2. There will be eating and drinking in the *kingdom of God.*
3. There will be eating and drinking in the *kingdom of Jesus.*
4 The *Father's* kingdom is everlasting!
5 *God's* kingdom is everlasting!
6 *Jesus'* kingdom is everlasting!

Is this a guessing game, or a wait-and-find-out which kingdom those who have eternal life will live in? Or is it possible that there is only ONE everlasting kingdom? Surprise! There are not many kingdoms. There is only one kingdom and it is for all who inherit eternal life. It is part of the gift of God that He has prepared for those who have put their trust and faith in Him. And *that kingdom*, will never end! Let's check it out.

> But the saints of the Most High shall receive *the kingdom*, and possess *the kingdom* forever, even forever and ever.
>
> —Dan. 7:18

> "Then the King (Jesus) will say to those on His right hand, come you blessed of My Father, inherit *the kingdom* prepared for you from the foundation of the world."
>
> —Matt. 25:34

> "Do not fear little flock, for it is your Father's good pleasure to give you *the kingdom*."
>
> —Luke 12:32

We are not looking at different types of kingdoms or one of several kingdoms. There is only one kingdom. It is referred to as "THE KINGDOM" (singular, not plural). Receive THE kingdom; possess THE kingdom; inherit THE kingdom; give you THE kingdom. It is not a variety of kingdoms. I am sure that much has been written and preached about this glorious, one and only, eternal kingdom, <u>but most important are the words of Jesus:</u>

"I go to prepare a place for you. And if I go and prepare a place for you, I will come again and receive you to Myself; that where I am, there you may be also."

—John 14:2-3

Wherever that place is, whatever that place is, trust Jesus; that is where you want to spend eternity.

Chapter Thirteen

Has Anyone Seen God?

NO! YES! -er- YES! NO! God is invisible! God is everywhere! God is Spirit!

This was not the easiest chapter to put on paper. I know what the Bible says, but communicating it was a challenge. I welcome all feedback on this subject or any portion of this book. An e-mail address is provided at the back of this book and I will attempt to respond to all, be it complementary or critical.

We are going to spend some time on this subject. It is a real eye-opener (pun intended), yet really fun to study. My intention is to use as many Bible passages as I can. I think by the end of this chapter, you will be convinced that humans have not and cannot physically see God, and you will equally be convinced that many humans indeed did physically see God.

There are some Scriptures in the Bible that seem on the surface to contradict each other, just as the last paragraph implies, however when you think (pray, study, research) the following Scriptures, they actually complement each other. Before we get started, let's look at another seemingly contradicting example in the Bible: How did Judas, the betrayer of Jesus die?

> Then he (Judas) threw down the pieces of silver in the temple and departed, and went and hanged himself.
>
> —Matt. 27:5

> ...He (Judas) burst open in the middle and all his entrails gushed out.
>
> —Acts 1:18

What we must realize is that God's Word is never wrong and never contradicts itself. The Bible does say that Judas did hang himself in Matthew and the book of Acts does say he burst open and spilled his guts out. This seems to be a contradiction but the Bible tells us that Judas died and both the hanging and the bursting did happen. Therefore, both accounts are true. Maybe in the process of hanging himself, the rope broke, maybe the branch broke, so that he hanged himself and also fell to the ground and burst open. Maybe he hung on the tree a day or two and somebody cut the rope and he fell to the ground and burst open. If the tree was over a cliff, he may have jumped and hit some sharp rocks and was cut open before he reached the end of the rope. Maybe while hanging, someone cut him open with a sword. If there seems to be a problem with interpretation, it lies with our lack of understanding, not God's Word.

So, if the Bible says no one has seen God at any time, then that has to be a 100% true statement. If the Bible seems to say the exact opposite and say that many people have seen God, then that also has to be 100% true! Our limited understanding, common sense, logic, and deductive reasoning can and does fall short at times, but with God's help there are answers. We will not always understand everything in the Bible, but we can trust that if God said it, it is true. Many times I believe God wants us to be curious enough to do some research and then God will say:

"Come now, and let us reason together," says the Lord.

—Isa. 1:18

"Your word is truth."

—John 17:17

"So I say to you, ask and it will be given to you; seek, and you will find; knock, and it will be opened to you."

—Luke 11:9

All scripture is given by inspiration of God and is profitable for doctrine, for reproof, for correction, for instruction in righteousness.

—2 Tim. 3:16

So, back to our question—Has anyone seen God?

No one has seen God at any time.

—John 1:18

...dwelling in unapproachable light, whom no man has seen or can see.

—1 Tim. 6:16

No one has seen God at any time.

—1 John 4:12

"Not that anyone has seen the Father."

—John 6:46

"And the Father Himself, who sent Me. You have never heard His voice at any time, nor seen His form.

—John 5:37

The Bible seems quite clear that human beings in our fallen state cannot see or even hear God. As we are soon to discover though, people did see God's form and hear his voice. Now let's remember that every Scripture that says people did not see God and every Scripture that says people did see God are both 100% true and accurate!

> But He (God) said, "*You cannot see My face*; for no man shall see Me, and live."
>
> —Exod. 33:20

Does this imply that God does have a face, but you will die if you see it?

> But since then there has not arisen in Israel a prophet like Moses, *whom the Lord knew face to face*.
>
> —Deut. 34:10

OOOPPPS! Face to face must be a misprint? Is this one of the apparent contradictions? "You cannot see my face and live" and "Whom the Lord knew face to face."

> And it came to pass, when Moses entered the tabernacle, that the pillar of cloud descended and stood at the door of the tabernacle, and *the Lord talked with Moses*. All the people saw the pillar of cloud standing at the tabernacle door, and all the people rose and worshiped, each man in his tent door. *So the Lord spoke to Moses face to face, as a man speaks to his friend.*
>
> —Exod. 33:9-11

This Scripture seems quite clear. When you talk to one of your friends face to face you can see them. As we will see later, this is not a dream or vision. In verse 10 it says that all the people saw the pillar of cloud from a distance and all the people worshiped from their tents. Worshiped whom? You don't worship a cloud and in fact you don't worship anyone less than God! The people knew God was there and Moses was close enough to see God face to face. Also, it is not a dream if all the people experience the same thing. If the encounter is a dream or vision the Scripture would tell us, as we are about to see. Also, there is no doubt that it is the Lord that is in the cloud. I believe the cloud is some type of restraint so that Moses can see God, but not in His full glory.

> Now the *Lord* descended in the cloud and *stood*
> *with him* there, and proclaimed the name of the
> Lord. And the *Lord passed before him* and pro-
> claimed, the Lord, the Lord God…
>
> —Exod. 34:5-6

If the Lord descended and stood with Moses, how did Moses know it was the Lord who descended and *stood* with him unless he could see the Lord? And why say "stood" instead of sitting or floating unless he really could see the Lord standing. Same question for the first sentence of the next verse.

> Then *the Lord came down* in the pillar of cloud
> *and stood in the door of the tabernacle*, and called

Aaron and Miriam. And they both went forward. Then He said, "Hear now My words; If there is a prophet among you, I, the Lord, make Myself known to him in a *vision*; I speak to him in a *dream. Not so with My servant Moses*; He is faithful in all My house. *I speak to him face to face*, Even plainly, and not in dark sayings; and *he sees the form of the Lord.*

—Num. 12:5-8

Many times God did communicate with people in dreams and visions, and if that was the case, the Bible makes that encounter very clear as we see in the last verse. There is an obvious difference between dream and vision, and face to face.

So Jacob called the name of the place Peniel: "For *I have seen God face to face, and my life is preserved.*"

—Gen. 32:30

Why would Jacob say, "and my life was preserved" if his encounter with God was a dream or vision, or he was just looking at a cloud? Actually, "face to face" is a very precise way to say you are actually, physically, in the presence of another person. I cannot think of many situations where I would be face to face with a friend or enemy and not see them. Has anyone ever "been in your face?" How close were they? At least in the same room and probably too close for comfort, I would guess.

If this encounter was a dream or vision the Bible would tells us so. Here are some examples of God communicating using dreams and visions.

> After these things the word of the Lord came to Abram in a *vision*, saying...
>
> —Gen. 15:1

> Then the Angel of God spoke to me in a *dream*, saying...
>
> —Gen. 31:11

> Then God spoke to Israel (Jacob's new name) in the *visions* of the night...
>
> —Gen. 46:2

> But God came to Abimelech in a *dream* by the night, and said to him...
>
> —Gen. 20:3

> And God said to him in a *dream*, "yes, I know that you did this in the integrity of your heart."
>
> —Gen. 20:6

> At Gibeon the Lord appeared to Solomon in a *dream* by night...
>
> —1 Kings 3:5

> Now the Lord spoke to Paul in the night by a *vision*...
>
> —Acts 18:9

And being warned by God in a dream...
—Matt. 2:22

Now there was a certain disciple at Damascus named Ananias; and to him the Lord said in a vision...
—Acts 9:10

The Bible has no problem telling us if we are reading about visions and dreams. Visions and dreams usually were not as fearful, yet when physically seeing and speaking to God, sometimes people were afraid and even thought they might die. The "face to face" was not a dream or vision, but rather it was, I am awake and this is real!

Then the *Lord appeared* to Abram and said, "to your descendants I will give this land." And there he built an altar to the *Lord who had appeared to him.*
—Gen. 12:7

Then she called the name of the Lord who spoke to her, "You-Are-the-God-Who-Sees;" for she said, " *Have I also here seen Him who sees me?*"
—Gen. 16:13

Then the eyes of both of them (Adam and Eve) were opened, and they knew that they were naked; and made themselves coverings. And they *heard the sound of the Lord God walking in the garden* in the cool of the day, and Adam and his wife hid themselves from the *presence of the Lord God among the trees of the garden.* Then the Lord God called to Adam and said to him, "Where are you?" so he said, "*I heard Your voice in the garden,* and I was afraid because I was naked; and I hid myself."

—Gen. 3:7-10

Adam and Eve covered themselves and hid because they knew that God was physically there. They were not hiding from themselves. They even *heard His footsteps walking in the garden.* Why would God allow the sound of His footsteps to be heard if He wasn't really there? Yes, Adam and Eve could both see and hear the God who created them. They did not want God to see them naked and God was the only one they could hide from, since they were the first two people to be created (no mention of children or other humans yet). And of course the Bible does tell us that they were "hiding from God."

And it came to pass, when Joshua was by Jericho, that he lifted his eyes and looked, and behold, a Man stood opposite him with His sword drawn in His hand. And Joshua went to Him and said to Him, "Are You for us or for our adversaries?" So He said, "No, but as Commander of the army of the Lord I have now come." And Joshua fell on his face to the earth and worshiped, and said to Him, "What does my Lord say to His servant?" Then the Commander of the Lord's army said to Joshua, "Take your sandal off your foot, for the place where you stand is holy." And Joshua did so.

—Josh. 5:13-15

Joshua sees a Man (face to face we are told) standing next to him with a visible sword. This Man claims to be the commander of the army of God (Jesus is in charge of the army of God.

Now *I saw heaven* opened, and behold, a white horse. And He (Jesus) who sat on him was called Faithful and True, and in righteousness *He judges and makes war.* And the armies in heaven, clothed in fine linen, white and clean, followed Him [Jesus] on white horses. And I saw the beast, the kings of the earth, and their armies, gathered together to make war against Him who sat on the horse and against His [Jesus'] army).

—Rev. 19:11 & 14 & 19

Joshua fell on his face and worshiped this Man (which is a sin, if it was a mortal man, ascended man, or an angel). This Man told Joshua to take off his sandals because he was on holy ground. The ground itself was not holy, but rather God (in the form of a Man) being present makes any ground holy. Another great example of holy ground is found in:

Then He (God) said, "Do not draw near this place. (Moses) Take your sandals off your feet, for the place where you stand is holy ground."

—Exod. 3:5

So, God and this Man with the sword both made the same claim about the holy ground. This Man with the sword proclaimed the ground to be holy and obviously the ground was not holy because Joshua was there. The only other person in close proximity was the man with the sword, who accepted worship from Joshua. Worship is to be accepted by Almighty God and Him alone.

And *the Lord appeared* to him the same night and said, "*I am the God* of your father Abraham."

—Gen. 26:24

Who is the God of Abraham? The Lord who appeared!

Then the *Lord appeared to him* (Isaac) and said: "Do not go down to Egypt; live in the land of which I will tell you. Dwell in this land, and I will be with you and bless you; for to you and your descendants I give all these lands, and I will perform the oath which I swore to Abraham your father. And I will make your descendants multiply as the stars of heaven; I will give to your descendants all these lands; and in your seed all the nations of the earth shall be blessed; because

Abraham obeyed *My voice* and kept *My charge,
My commandments, My statutes,* and *My laws.*"
—Gen. 26:2-5

The *Lord that appeared and spoke* to Isaac had to
be God. Only God could make Isaac's descendants
multiply as the stars of heaven. The oath sworn to
Abraham was performed by God because Abraham
obeyed God's voice, charge, commandments, statutes, and laws.

I want to include the next chapter in it's entirety.
A good author/ preacher could stay in this chapter a
month of Sundays and not run out of inspirational
subject matter. Pay close attention to the interac-
tion between the Lord (who is God) and Abraham.
I know this is a very serious chapter, but also there
is some humor and much sharing of thoughts and
feelings on a very personal, verbal, visible level.

Then the *Lord appeared* to him (Abraham) by
the terebinth trees of Mamre, as he was sitting in
the tent door in the heat of the day. So he lifted
his eyes and looked, and behold, *three men* were
standing by him, and when he saw them, he ran
from the tent door to meet them, and bowed himself to the ground and said, "My Lord, if I have
now found favor in Your sight, do not pass on by
Your servant. Please let a little water be brought,
and wash Your feet, and rest yourselves under the
tree. And I will bring a morsel of bread, that you
may refresh your hearts. After that you may pass

by, inasmuch as you have come to your servant." They said, "Do as you have said." So Abraham hurried into the tent to Sarah and said, "Quickly, make ready three measures of fine meal; knead it and make cakes." And Abraham ran to the herd, took a tender and good calf, gave it to a young man, and he hastened to prepare it. So he took butter and milk and the calf which he had prepared, and set it before them; and he stood by them under the tree *as they ate.* Then they said to him, "where is Sarah your wife?" So he said, "Here, in the tent." And He said, I will certainly return to you according to the time of life, and behold, Sarah your wife shall have a son." (Sarah was listening in the tent door which was behind him.) Now Abraham and Sarah were old, well advanced in age; and Sarah had passed the age of childbearing. Therefore *Sarah laughed within herself*, saying, "After I have grown old, shall I have pleasure, my lord (husband) being old also?" And the Lord said to Abraham, "Why did Sarah laugh, saying, "Shall I surely bear a child, since I am old?" *Is anything too hard for the Lord?* At the appointed time I will return to you, according to the time of life, and Sarah shall have a son." But Sarah denied it, saying, "I did not laugh," for she was afraid. And He said, "No but you did laugh!" Then the men rose from there and looked toward Sodom, and Abraham went with them to send them on their way. And the Lord said, "Shall I hide from Abraham what I am doing, since Abraham shall surely become a great and mighty nation, and all the nations of the earth shall be blessed in him?" For I have known him, in order that he may command his children and his household after him, that they keep the way of the Lord, to do righteousness and justice, that the Lord may bring to Abraham what He has spoken to him." And the Lord said, "Because the outcry against Sodom and Gomorrah is great, and because their sin is very grave, I will go down now and see whether they have done altogether according to the outcry against it that has come to Me; and if not, I will know." Then *the men* turned away from there and went toward Sodom, but Abraham still stood before the Lord. And Abraham came near and said, "Would You also destroy the righteous with the wicked? Suppose there were fifty righteous within the city; would You also destroy the place and not spare it for the fifty righteous that were in it? Far be it from You to do such a thing as this, to slay the righteous with the wicked, so that the righteous should be as the wicked; far be it from You! *Shall not the Judge of all the earth do right?*" So the Lord said, If I find in Sodom fifty righteous within the city, then I will spare all the place for their sakes." Then Abraham answered and said, "Indeed now, I who am but dust and ashes have taken it upon myself to speak to the Lord: Suppose there were five less than the fifty righteous; would You destroy all of the city for the lack of five?" So He said "If I find there forty-five, I will not destroy it." And he spoke to Him yet again and said, "Suppose there should be forty found there?" So He said, "I will not do it for the sake of the forty." Then he said, "Let not the Lord be angry, and I will speak: Suppose thirty should be found there?" So He said, "I will not do it if I find thirty there." And he said, "Indeed now, I have taken it upon myself to speak to the Lord: Suppose twenty should be found there?" So He said, "I will not destroy it for the sake of the twenty." Then he said, "Let not the Lord be angry, and I will speak but once more: Suppose ten should be found there?" And He said, I will not destroy it for the sake of ten." So the *Lord went His way* as soon as He had finished speaking with Abraham; and Abraham returned to his place.

—Gen. 18:1-33

Back to verse one, "the Lord appeared." As we read in Genesis 17:1..."The *Lord appeared…and said, I am God Almighty*." So the Lord that Abraham is seeing is *God Almighty*. Abraham saw the Lord next to a tree. The Lord rested under the tree. The Lord's feet were washed by Abraham (or a servant). The Lord and two others are called "men." So they have the outward appearance of humans.

One man is the Lord, the other two are angels (Gen. 19:1 Now the two angels came to Sodom in the evening, and Lot was sitting in the gate of Sodom. *When Lot saw them, he rose to meet them*). Sometimes angels are seen as truly magnificent, strong, and beautiful beings. Sometimes they appear as normal men as we just read in Genesis chapter 19 (read verses 1 to 12 for a better understanding). Also consider…

"Do not forget to entertain strangers, for by so do-ing some have unwittingly entertained angels."
—Hebrews 13:2

So all three looked like men, but Abraham knew it was his Lord and he was the servant. Abraham asked if he could feed them a morsel of bread (small portion of food). The answer was yes. Sarah, his wife, ground some wheat or other grain, mixed water and other ingredients, mixed it together and baked it (it takes me all day to make and bake bread). Abraham had a calf killed, then prepared and cooked it. Then Abraham brought the bread, meat (yes, *red meat*, and the Lord and angels ate it) and butter and milk. Then *Abraham watched the Lord and two angels eat,* as they sat under a tree. Sounds more like a feast than a "morsel" of food. I am sure Abraham wanted to offer the Lord the best of what he had. It is quite clear that this is not a dream! There is no indica-tion that this event is anything but real. Abraham, Sarah, and most likely some of their servants saw this man (in appearance) physically, yet it was the Lord God Almighty.

God had just told Abraham in the last chapter (Gen. 17) that he and Sarah would have a child, but because of their age, Abraham laughed. Then, The Lord again told Abraham that he and Sarah would have a child (chapter 18). This time Sarah heard the Lord and she also laughed, quietly to herself. Even though she wasn't laughing out loud, the Lord heard her laugh in her mind and told her so. The

Lord also told them when this child would be born, that it would be a boy, and they were to name him Isaac. Then, right at the time of birth, He would return to see them again (Gen. chapter 21). Then the Lord tells them that nothing is too hard for Him. Please remember, Abraham and Sarah are seeing a man in their presence. He was eating, drinking, sitting, walking, talking, and proclaiming prophesies to them, face to face; He also claimed that nothing was too hard for Him to do! Sounds like a claim only God could make, wouldn't you agree?

Next, these three men are on their way to Sodom and Gomorrah to destroy these cities. Abraham had no doubts whatsoever that they had the power to destroy entire cities and would destroy these cities if they chose to. In fact, Abraham addresses this Man before him as "the Judge of all the earth." Only God can be the Judge of all the earth! Abraham persuaded the Lord not to destroy these cities if He could find ten righteous men (down from fifty righteous men) because Lot, his nephew, lived there. The Lord sent the two angels into the city to talk to Lot, yet they were seen by everyone as normal men, not angels. The angles did not find even ten righteous men, but they did tell Lot and his family to get out. Then…

Then the Lord rained brimstone and fire on Sodom and Gomorrah.

—Gen. 19:24

This was the same Lord (in appearance as a man) that Abraham sat with, fed, washed His feet, talked to, and was told prophesies that did indeed come true. This was the same Lord who claimed He was God Almighty. It would take some power to call down fire and brimstone from the sky and control where it hit. Wouldn't you agree? Today we have computers and big bombs that are capable of that, but back then such was not the case.

> And Abraham went early in the morning to the place where *he had stood before the Lord.* Then he looked toward Sodom and Gomorrah, and toward all the land of the plain; and he saw, and behold, the smoke of the land which went up like the smoke of a furnace. And it came to pass, when _God destroyed the cities of the plain..._
>
> —Gen. 19:27-29

So, who destroyed Sodom and Gomorrah? Well, the Lord did, a Man did, and so did God! All are one and the same. The Man is the Lord, the Lord is Jesus, Jesus is God, and God is God Almighty. As we read earlier:

> "I am the Lord, and there is no other; there is no God besides Me."
>
> —Isa. 45:5

Some people of various religious persuasions (although professing the Bible as the Word of God), might say, "it was not *God Almighty* that these people were seeing, but angels or a man that God gave *su-*

pernatural powers to. As we have just read, that is not what the Bible plainly declares. However, if that line of thinking is pursued, anyone believing that line of thinking will need a pair of scissors, so they can cut these next passages out of their Bible.

> When Abram was ninety-nine years old, *the Lord appeared* to Abram and said to him, "*I am Almighty God*, walk before Me and be blameless."
> —Gen. 17:1

> Then *God appeared* to Jacob again, when he came from Padan Aram, and blessed him. Also *God said to him: "I am God Almighty…"*
> —Gen. 35:9 & 11

> Then Jacob said to Joseph: "*God Almighty appeared to me* at Luz in the land of Canaan and blessed me…"
> —Gen. 48:3

> And God spoke to Moses and said to him: "*I am the Lord. I appeared* to Abraham, to Isaac, and to Jacob, *as God Almighty…*"
> —Exod. 6:2-3

> Moreover He said "I am the God of your father, the God of Abraham, the God of Isaac, and the God of Jacob." And Moses hid his face, for he was afraid to look upon God.
> —Exod. 3:6

There is but one conclusion: the Lord is God and God is God Almighty, which also means God Almighty is the Lord and the Lord was walking, talking, and eating as He visibly interacted with many people. God was in human form. It could only be Jesus!

Ok! Back to the title of this chapter, Has Anyone Seen God? God is Spirit and God is unapproachable light. God is everywhere at the same time. God is in the past, the present, and the future. I *personally* don't know if we will ever, throughout eternity, see God or ever comprehend everything about God. If we knew everything that God knows, we would be God. I doubt that God in His full glory can be seen or ever will be seen, however that is just my opinion. God in His full glory is unapproachable light. Some may argue that the unapproachable light may be approachable in Heaven. On the other side of the answer to this question, as you have read over and over in this book, Jesus is fully God, the exact representation of God. Because Jesus is God, if you are looking at Jesus you are seeing God; if you are talking to Jesus, you are talking to God. All of the physical appearances we have just studied, which include the Lord, or God, or the Almighty, is Jesus! God in three Persons, Father, Son, Holy Spirit, all are the one and only eternal God. Jesus said:

"He that has seen Me, has seen the Father."
—John 14:9

" I and My Father are one."

—John 10:30

And then these Scriptures leave us no choice but to believe that Jesus is truly God!

For in Him (Jesus) dwells all the fullness of the Godhead bodily.

—Col. 2:9

…Christ, the *power of God* and the *wisdom of God.*

—1 Cor. 1:24

…Christ, who is the *image of God.*

—2 Cor. 4:4

He (Jesus) is the image of the *invisible God*…For by Him all things were created that are in heaven and that are on the earth, visible and *invisible*…All things were created through Him and for Him.

—Col. 1:15-17

Notice that Jesus created *all things* and some of that is invisible. There is a part of creation that is invisible. It's very possible that the invisible part of creation may be the biggest part of creation. The evolutionists don't have a clue, do they? A Scripture that fits them well is:

"Professing to be wise, they became fools."

—Rom. 1:22

God the Father and God the Holy Spirit are invisible, yet if you see Jesus, you see the exact representation of God, bodily.

If Jesus created all things, He also created Abraham. Jesus even told us that He existed before Abraham...

"...Abraham rejoiced to see My day and he saw it and was glad." Then the Jews said to Him, "You are not yet fifty years old, and *have You seen Abraham?*" Jesus said to them, "Most assuredly, I say to you, before Abraham was, I AM."

—John 8:56-58

Here we see the "I AM" claim again! Jesus is telling them "before Abraham was born, I AM God"! The Jews knew Jesus was claiming to be God and He also was stating that He and Abraham knew each other face to face. I don't know how much Abraham knew about Jesus as in the New Testament Jesus. I doubt he knew Him by the name of Jesus, however Abraham did know Him as God and as "the Judge of all the earth." Jesus was the one who appeared to Abraham, ate his food, talked to Sarah, and told them of a son they would have in the next year. Jesus is also the one who destroyed Sodom and Gomorrah. Jesus created all things, including the Garden of Eden. Jesus is the one who walked in the garden with Adam and Eve. Some day (maybe soon) Christians will walk and talk with Jesus in a new Garden of Eden! I wonder if we will have to wait in line to talk to him?

So, can God be seen? As unapproachable light, NO! Yet when we see Jesus, we see God face to face!

The next chapter is just a little glimpse as to what the Father, Jesus, and the Holy Spirit created!

Chapter Fourteen

Where Did It Start?

"In the beginning God created the heavens and the earth."

—Gen. 1:1

Dwell on that very long and it will test your sanity. So where did God come from? Why did God create the heavens and the earth? Has God always existed? What is God like? Can we know Him? Is there an answer for every question? I am sure God has an answer for every question and in time God will reveal all the answers we seek. I have questions about time, "outer space," and the universe. I will be the first to admit I probably shouldn't attempt my insights on such subjects, but then again why not?

This book is not about quoting movie stars, but maybe I can get away with just one. The quote was something like: "Truth, you can't handle the truth." Living in this world is like living in a very small, lid on the top, box. The truth is, we are not ready for all the truth, but truth is coming and it will be revealed in eternity. For example, we have a color spectrum that we can see, red, blue, green, yellow, and many other colors, but how many colors does God know about that He hasn't revealed yet? Well, infra-red and ultra-violet are two colors that we know exist, but the human eye can't see, and I know there are more, probably millions or billions of colors. What a light show God is preparing for us!

Dogs not only have better hearing than humans, but they can also hear sounds beyond our ability as well. A silent dog whistle can be tuned for their ears and not ours. A choir of angels could be in a room and sing your dog to glorious contentment, and musically lull him to sleep and you most likely would not hear one heavenly note. How much sound, how much music are we missing out on now? The time is coming though when our senses and our minds will be greatly increased. The place is called heaven, and the time will be when we see Jesus. Are you ready? Are you willing?

Well, does God even exist? If you have read this far, I am sure you believe God exists or you would be occupying your time with something else by now. But what about the person who says, "What If God does not exist? Let's follow that line of thinking back aways starting with, where did you come from? You are an offspring of your parents of course! Where did your parents come from? Where did your great, great grandparents come from? You can try to follow that line of thinking till you get all the way back to monkeys, then sea creatures, then a pond of slime. Then this pond of slime may have been struck by a bolt of lightning to create the first living cell (life from non-life? And atheists think Christians are crazy to have faith in a Creator? PLEASE!). Where did the water come from? Where did the slime come from? Where did the lightning come from? Where did the earth come from?

Well, there is a theory (not even close to fact) that is called evolution. It is taught in our public schools as truth, and is similar to this: There was a solid mass out there somewhere in space that always existed. It never had a beginning (blind faith based on dirt, water, and energy that always existed?). One day (except there were no days, so once upon a time) this solid mass heated up and exploded and created the universe. How could this solid mass have always existed? And even if it did always exist, what caused it to heat up? Why did it not heat up and explode billions of years earlier? When it exploded how did it create the universe? Where did the gas come from that all the stars need to stay burning? Where did the matches come from to light the stars on fire? And anyway, that would have been quite an explosion to create a universe that seems to have a magnificent and consistent design. Most of the time we think of explosions as chaotic, disorderly, and destructive. All by chance or an accident, you ask? Please! It is easier and more logical to believe in creation by a supreme intelligence, even if you don't believe in the God of the Bible, than random chance, even though we can't comprehend either one.

So, just how big is the "created" universe? The answer is that we don't know. I might be able to demonstrate how big a part of the "known" universe is, though. I'd like to use the speed of light as a measuring stick. Light travels approximimtely186,282 miles per second. If you had a beam of light that could circle the earth, it would go around the earth seven and one half times in one second (obviously you know it takes about one second to say "one thousand one" out loud). At that same speed, it takes light over eight minutes to travel from the sun to the earth. Our sun is one of millions of suns (stars) in our galaxy, which is called the Milky Way. Every star you see at night is in our Milky Way galaxy. It takes light one hundred thousand *years*, traveling at 186,282 miles per second, to cross the expanse of our average sized galaxy, and our galaxy is just a dot compared to the size the universe. Scientists estimate there are a million galaxies (one hundred thousand light years across) inside the cup of the big dipper, if you go out into the universe far enough, and possibly billions of galaxies in the universe. And let me ask, who is to say God only has one universe? Maybe there are invisible universes that are part of God's invisible creation that we read about earlier. I cannot comprehend the size of the universe, however, I do know the universe exists. I cannot comprehend God, but I know He exists. There is proof of God's existence in creation, in true science, nature, and logic and there are lots of great books available on this subject, so if you enjoy that kind of information, read to your heart's content. Fill your mind with knowledge of God (Matt. 7:7 "...seek and you will find..."). There is a God-created vacuum in your life. Let God fill it His way. God gave us His Word, the Bible. It is His truth! All truth comes from God!

We really only have two choices as to our existence:

1. creation by chance or,
2. creation by intelligence.

Either the mass of the universe has always existed on its own and created itself or God has always existed and created the universe and everything in it. Both take faith, both will stretch your mind beyond your mental limits. If you believe life created itself, get all you can, any way you can, as fast as you can, for life is short and after all, you are accountable to no one. If however, God created everything and He says He has a plan for your life and it is a perfect and spectacular plan, you might want to check it out (I mean really check it out). How eternally tragic it would be to reject this "eternal life" plan with not much more than a passing glance or a joke or two. If there is a hereafter, (heaven and hell) it just might last for a long, long time!

Chapter Fifteen

What Is the Will?

In life we have many choices. We have a desire, a drive, a passion, a wish list, if you will, to do what we choose. That is our will. Most of our life we make choices and then live by the choices we make. Sometimes we try to change or undo our choices. Sometimes others make choices for us; even so, we can usually make choices concerning their choices (lunch break only at 11:30 AM or 1:30 PM, pay/don't pay, Quit/don't quit, Strike back/don't strike back, hot or cold, maybe I will, maybe later, maybe never, I will get even, etc.).

Lots of choices are fun and/or easy. Some are hard and/or difficult. One choice is eternal (heaven or hell). The simple part of that choice is that there are only two choices. The truth is that we all must make our eternal choice <u>in this life</u>. God created most of us to have the ability to choose by using our will. He wants us to choose to trust Him in all things. Accept Jesus as your personal Savior (heaven) or reject Him (hell). Not choosing Jesus is a choice that equals rejecting Jesus. That is not a popular belief, but it is the spoken words of Jesus Himself:

> "He that is not with Me is against Me…"
> —Matt. 12:30

> "…for if you do not believe that I am He, you will die in your sins."
> —John 8:24

If you are not saved, you are lost—there is no in-between. By your will, if you reject the truth, you choose to be *willingly ignorant.* I want to restate this eternal truth. *If you are ignorant of the love of God and the salvation God has provided, it is by choice.* In this country and many other countries, there are churches in every town and city that teach the truth (though not all) about eternal life.

The Bible is in every bookstore, grocery store, K-Mart, Target, Wal-Mart, second hand stores, etc. Almost every home and most hotels and motels have Bibles. God's Word is everywhere. There are more Bibles in the world than any other book. As I have stated before, the Bible is the most published book of all recorded history. Bibles are given away free to those who will ask.

I would dare to say most people have family, friends, or neighbors who know the truth and are willing to share about God's love, forgiveness, and salvation. I hope you are either sharing God's truth or diligently seeking His truth. God is seeking you. If you are willing, God will find you! In fact, God knows you before you are willing and His promise to us is that He is not far off.

The question always comes up, "What about the person who lives in an isolated village or a person with a low I.Q.?" First of all, you and I do not qualify in those situations. We are personally responsible for what God has provided for us. And we are surrounded by God's truth. As for the people in the isolated village or who have a low I.Q., that is God's problem and God will be fair with them. He is a loving and just God. He knows how to deal with those situations with absolute fairness and we will do well to trust Him in all things. OK, back to "willingly ignorant."

And with all unrighteous deception among those who perish, because *they did not receive the love of the truth*, that they might be saved. That they all may be condemned *who did not believe the truth* but had pleasure in unrighteousness.
— 2 Thess. 2:10 & 12

"Did not receive the truth" means it was offered and rejected. "Did not believe the truth" means it was told, but not accepted. These are obviously choices of the will. There are many more Scriptures to consider because God is not bored with repeating Himself. God does use repetition to make His points crystal clear. In fact, as you are about to see, God is a huge supporter of repetition—especially concerning our God-given ability to choose.

> For the time will come when *they will not endure sound doctrine*, but according <u>*to their own desires*</u>, because they have itching ears, they will heap up for themselves teachers; and *they will turn from the truth*, and be turned aside to fables.
>
> —2 Tim. 4:3-4

"Will not endure sound doctrine" means *choosing* not to tolerate sound doctrine. Because of "their own desires (their will) they will turn from the truth." The truth is there, but they turn away by *choice*.

> …not giving heed to Jewish fables and commandments of *men who turn from the truth*.
>
> —Titus 1:14

There are men who "choose to turn from the truth." We can choose not to believe men who turn from the truth. But how do we know what truth is, unless we can define truth? Truth is conformity with fact. The next two Scriptures tell us exactly what truth is:

Your righteousness is an everlasting righteousness, and *Your law is truth.*

—Ps. 119:142

"Sanctify them by Your truth. *Your word is truth.*"

—John 17:17

I think the definition of "truth" we are seeking is: God's *law is truth* and God's *Word is truth.* If you study your Bible, you will also know who the men are who turn from the truth. You don't have to look very hard to see the results of men who have rejected God's truth. Always compare what men say (including this author) against the Bible. Truth will never contradict the Bible!

"But *you are not willing* to come to Me that you may have life.

—John 5:40

"Not willing" is a choice of the will to reject eternal life.

"And this is the condemnation, that the light has come into the world, and *men loved darkness* rather than the light."

—John 3:19

The light is God's truth. It is in the world. Men love darkness (sin) rather than the truth. Yes, love darkness! The end result of sin is repulsive and painful but in the beginning sin can be fun, exciting, mysterious, and enticing.

Sin is like a mouse trap and the fun is the cheese or peanut butter in the middle. We may think we can "get away" with a nibble, but that nibble attempts to entice us back. Sin can start out seemingly easy or innocent; however, sometimes the mouse trap of sin gets a leg or an eye. Sometimes sin develops into a sore, infection, or disease. Obviously, bad things can happen when you don't sin or other people's sins can affect you as well, because sin is in the world and we all are born with a sin nature. Committing sin does increase the odds of being affected by it though. Sin might lead us to an addiction that we reasoned could never actually control us. The end result of sin always causes death. That is why Jesus needs to wash away our sin.

Satan and his demons are masters at deception and without Jesus we don't have a chance. If your hand doesn't belong in someone else's cookie jar, watch out for the "hidden mouse trap." The SNAP can be loud and public or silent and deadly. A mouse trap in a cookie jar sounds like a stupid example. However, the point is, sin can find you when and where you least expect it and you don't expect a mouse trap in a cookie jar. Sin usually comes back on us in a way we didn't plan, or in a manner we didn't dream we could be caught. Sometimes we justify sin, thinking nobody will really get hurt. I am sure you can think of some sin you have been involved in, that came back to bite you in a way that surprised you. Welcome to the club to which we all belong ! God's answer to sin…

> "For God so loved the world that He gave His only begotten Son, that <u>whoever believes</u> in Him should not perish but have everlasting life."
>
> —John 3:16

"Whoever believes" means anyone and everyone. It is our choice to have eternal life through the finished work of Jesus.

> "Today, *if you will hear* His voice, *do not harden* your hearts."
>
> —Heb. 4:7

The word "If" in the last quote is another one of those small, seemingly insignificant words that has a big meaning. "If" implies a condition or a choice. God is saying to us, it is your choice, please listen, do not choose to reject the truth that the Holy Spirit of God is revealing to you.

I am by no means saying you can choose God's plan of salvation on your own. God will first approach you through the Bible, a friend, a preacher, a tragedy in your life, a book, a song, a dream, a movie, or many other methods. Then, God will expose your eternally lost condition, your need for forgiveness, and the plan of salvation through Jesus Christ. He has the plan. He has done the work. Our choice is to accept or reject God's plan of salvation.

> And the world is passing away, and the lust of it; but *he who does the will* of God abides forever.
>
> —1 John 2:17

And again, "he who does the will of God" is making a choice. I might add that if you make (or have already made) the right choice, you will be with God forever in a sin-free heaven. Amen!

> *Whoever denies* the Son does not have the Father either; *he who acknowledges* the Son has the Father also.
>
> —1 John 2:23

"Whoever denies" and "he who acknowledges" are both choices of our will.

From the very beginning of His ministry, Jesus preached choice. He told us to repent and choose to follow Him. He also told us the consequences of choosing not to follow Him.

> From that time Jesus began to preach and to say, "Repent, for the kingdom of heaven is at hand."
>
> —Matt. 4:17

> "I tell you no; but *unless you repent* you will all likewise perish."
>
> —Luke 13:3

Unless you repent! No one can do that for you! It is your choice, your will. For most people it is the hardest, easiest choice you will ever make.

And the Spirit and the bride say, "Come!" And let him who hears say, "Come!" And let him who thirsts come. *Whoever desires*, let him take of the water of life freely.

—Rev. 22:17

The word "come" is another simple everyday word, yet one of the most *important* words in the Bible. It is an invitation for eternal life. And again, it offers us a choice. Jesus said:

"*Come to Me*, all you who labor and are heavy laden, and I will give you rest."

—Matt. 11:28

but these (scriptures) are written that you may believe that Jesus is the Christ, the Son of God, and that believing you may have life in His name.

—John 20:31

But without faith it is impossible to please Him, for he who comes to God must believe that He is, and that He is a rewarder of those who diligently seek Him.

—Heb. 11:6

Have you made your choice? "Whoever desires" is an open invitation to all of mankind. It is so tragic that many people will reject this gift of eternal life or *just choose not to choose*. I wonder why we, as human beings, are given the truth, we are capable of freely choosing eternal life or eternal death and so many choose death willingly? God says it over and over and over and over and over; eternal life is only through Jesus Christ and it is a choice of the will. If God is speaking to you, CHOOSE LIFE! If you haven't made the decision to accept Jesus Christ as your personal Savior but would like to, read on.

Chapter Sixteen

What Is Salvation and Eternal Life? (Option One!)

God's salvation is deliverance and forgiveness from all sin and eternal punishment through the death and resurrection of the Lord Jesus Christ. All humans have sin in their lives. We are born with a sin nature. Some people sin more than others; however just ONE sin is enough to keep you out of heaven. Commit one sin and you need the blood of Jesus to pay the price for that sin. His perfect blood can wash away that sin (and all sins in your life).

With an honest look at our lives (and others' as well) no one has committed just one sin, but rather so many, it is not possible to even keep count (I am pointing a finger at me). Only through Jesus can our sins be forgiven. If however, we narrow sin down to just one, the sin of rejecting salvation through Jesus Christ cannot be forgiven after you die. If you die without Jesus, you do not get a second chance. I must admit I am not comfortable with that but, it is Biblical fact. I know people that I really like and people that I really love, who I assume (though I am not their judge) are not "born-again" Christians. I miss them painfully already, if they are not headed in the direction of heaven. However, these are God's terms, God's laws, not mine.

My personal commitment is to:

Trust in the Lord with all your heart, and lean not on your own understanding; In all your ways acknowledge Him, and He shall direct your paths.

—Prov. 3:5-6

If you can find a way around these next few Scriptures, let me know what that way might be.

"He who believes in the Son has everlasting life; and he who does not believe the Son shall not see life…"

—John 3:36

"Nor is there salvation in any other (Jesus), for there is no other name under heaven given among men (women) by which we MUST BE SAVED."

—Acts 4:12

This has been said before, but it needs to be repeated: JESUS IS NOT A WAY YOU MIGHT BE

SAVED! JESUS IS NOT ONE OF SEVERAL WAYS TO BE SAVED. JESUS IS THE *ONLY* WAY YOU MUST BE SAVED!

> ...If you confess with your mouth the Lord Jesus and believe in your heart that God has raised Him from the dead, you will be saved. For with the heart one believes unto righteousness, and with the mouth confession is made unto salvation. For "*Whoever* calls on the name of the Lord shall be saved."
>
> —Rom. 10:9-10 & 13

> "For God so loved the world that He gave His only begotten Son, that <u>whoever</u> believes in Him should not perish but have everlasting life."
>
> —John 3:16

We are of course listening to God tell us about our will to choose. We just looked at "choice" in the last chapter. I have heard it said about some people that they "got religion" just before they died. I would hope for their sake that means they accepted Jesus Christ as their personal Savior. Because, as we read in the last few Scriptures above, religion will never get even one person to heaven, only Jesus can do that!

Salvation through Jesus is instantaneous! Accept Jesus, and you instantly pass from death to life. The thief on the cross next to Jesus is a good example of a last minute or deathbed salvation. He had no time for baptism, no time to make things right with people he had wronged, no time to stop bad habits, no time to change his lifestyle or become religious. He did by choice place his faith and trust in Jesus. Salvation came to this sinner "on the spot"—one moment in time changed his destiny and he is now enjoying eternal life and will forever.

An interesting side note about the thief on the cross. This man did have a short but powerful personal testimony and it is still being heard today. He asked Jesus publicly to save him and instantly Jesus said "today you will be with Me in paradise." That is in the Bible and it is read everyday by someone who needs to hear his simple, from the heart, plea for forgiveness. I really believe that man will be rewarded every time his testimony is used to lead another person to salvation in Jesus.

However, not all of us will get a few minutes or hours to get right with God before death, as the thief on the cross did. That is not a safe bet or a risk worth taking, when we are talking about our eternal future. If you think you can wait till the last minute of your life and then call out to Jesus, that is not logical. Besides, If you think you would call out to Jesus in your last moments that means you already assume He is the way, the truth, and the life. You are just choosing not to trust Him as your personal Savior at this time. But, if He is the only way, why put it off? The Bible says:

> Behold, now is the accepted time; behold *now is the day of salvation.*
>
> —2 Cor. 6:2

Why today and not tomorrow? Some people die in their sleep, and car accidents happen way too fast. Sometimes people wake up in a hospital and don't even know what happened to them. Some people are taken to the hospital for a small problem, put to sleep, but they don't wake up! I'm not saying "don't trust hospitals," but rather be ready to meet God whether you are awake or asleep. The point is you may or may not know when you will die, but the odds so far are running at about 100% that your day is coming. There are a hundred ways to die, but only two places you can go. If you are a Christian reading this, you know about the hope and comfort that is within you. You don't have all the answers, but you know that God does and when your last breath is drawn, whether you are awake or asleep, God will take care of you.

If you have not accepted Jesus as your personal Savior, there are no excuses to put it off. Down deep you know the truth! You have been reading the truth in this book, as best as I can express it. Put your trust in Jesus now and you will be eternally blessed. A simple prayer from your heart might be something like:

God, thank You for loving me so much. I ask You to forgive me for all the sin in my life and all the wrong things I've done. Thank You for sending Jesus to die for my sins. I choose to invite You to come into my life. Help me become the person You created me to be. Remember me, just like You remembered the thief on the cross who put his trust in You. Thank You, in Jesus' name, amen.

This is "the narrow gate" mentioned earlier and If you just prayed a prayer something like this, from your heart, you passed through that gate!!! Tell somebody whom you believe to be a Christian. They will rejoice with you. They were probably praying for you to "get saved" in the first place and you just did! Even the angels of heaven will be rejoicing with you. Now you can seek God's will for your life! And please do remember to pray and share your faith with family and friends that need Jesus. Heaven is a big place and there is lots of room for everybody.

Chapter Seventeen

What Is Salvation and Eternal Life? (Option Two? Same as Option One!)

For I am not ashamed of the gospel of Christ, for it is the power of God to salvation for everyone who believes…

—Rom. 1:16

For the message of the cross is foolishness to those who are perishing, but to us who are being saved it is the power of God.

—1 Cor. 1:18

A very rich man of our present time said (this is not an exact quote, but it's close) "I'm sure Jesus was a good man, did lots of good things, but I don't need Him dying on a cross for me." WRONG! The Bible says that man is a fool! He will die (eternally) in his sin unless he changes his mind about the victory Jesus accomplished at the cross and then ask

145

Jesus to save him. Even if this man became so rich that he would be the richest most powerful man alive, then he gave 99% of his wealth to the poor, the sick, and the hungry and lived on just 1% of his wealth, if he dies without Jesus, he will not have eternal life. Because:

> "For what profit is it to a man if he gains the whole world, and loses his own soul? Or what will a man give in exchange for his soul?"
> —Matt. 16:26

The shed blood of Jesus is the only thing God will accept in exchange for a condemned soul. There are not enough good works in the whole world to save even one person.

> *Not by works* of righteousness which *we have done*, but according to his mercy He saved us…
> —Titus 3:5

> *For by grace you have been saved through faith, and that not of yourselves; it is the gift of God not of works, lest anyone should boast.*
> —Eph. 2:8-9

Not one person in heaven is going to be able to say, "look what I did to get here." Every person in heaven will say, "look what Jesus did to get me here." If you are a Christian, yes, there will be rewards in heaven for good works done here on earth, but we must not confuse "heavenly rewards" with the "free gift of God's grace" of eternal life!

Let's take a quick look at "heavenly rewards." First, heavenly rewards are only for Christians. You have to already be a Christian before you can start earning heavenly rewards. Yes, you can earn them, and yes they are important and we are encouraged to work for them in a way that would please God. Second, Christians can lose rewards and still have eternal life.

> If anyone's work which he has built on it endures, he will receive a reward. If anyone's work is burned, he will suffer loss; but he himself will be saved...
>
> —1 Cor. 3:14-15

> Look to yourselves that we do not lose those things we worked for, but that we may receive a *full reward*.
>
> —2 John v. 8

Remember, we work for rewards to more fully enjoy heaven. The Bible tells us our reward can be full, part, or nothing. Eternal life (going to heaven) is a free gift if you choose to accept it. It is not based on works, so that no one in heaven can boast.

> "For the Son of Man will come in the glory of His Father with His angels, and then He will reward each according to his works."
>
> —Matt. 16:27

"For whoever gives you a cup of water to drink in My name, *because you belong to Christ*, assuredly, I say to you, he will by no means lose his reward."

—Mark 9:41

Yes, there are tons of rewards for good works done here on earth. Imagine receiving a heavenly blessing for even giving someone a cup of water. Hey, by all means hand out a million cups of *cool* water in the name of Jesus, but don't try to use any (or all) of your works to get in to heaven. God will only accept the work of Jesus Christ as your acceptance through the pearly gates. The subject of heavenly rewards is a book in itself and there are many good books written on the subject, so enough from me.

I am sure that not one reader of this book could miss the importance of Jesus Christ—who He is and what He did for us. Christians are accused of being narrow-minded because we believe salvation is through Jesus Christ alone, and so we are, by choice, only because the Bible says:

He who has the Son has life; he who does not have the Son of God does not have life.

—1 John 5:12

If you are a Christian and are wrongly accused because you accept God's Word as the gospel truth, praise God for who He is, then pray earnestly for the people who condemn you. God hates (yes, God is capable of hating) sin, but loves the sinner. We all fall short of perfection and we all need prayer support from other Christians every day. May God's will be done!

We as Christians are not yet perfect, but praise God, we are forgiven and have been adopted into the family of God. In fact the only way we can be in the family of God is to be adopted.

One final thought on the triune God (Father, Son, and the Holy Spirit): At the creation of man...

> Then God said, "Let *Us* make man in *Our* image, according to *Our* likeness..."
>
> —Gen. 1:26

Notice that God is speaking and says "Let Us" and "Our image" and "Our likeness." "Us" and "Our" are plural and mean more than one. More than one what? There is only one God and yet God is referred to as a plural being. The interpretation means that the Father, the Son, and the Holy Spirit all participated in creation. Three Persons equal the one God. I can only make a feeble attempt at explaining the Trinity, but that has not been the goal of this book. Rather, the point is that God says He eternally exists in "three Persons" and Jesus is one person of the Trinity. That has been the main focus of this book! Can we completely understand that? No! Is it proclaimed throughout the Old Testament and the New Testament? Yes! Exercise your faith in God to believe what He has revealed to you. Understand what you can. Realize you can't comprehend God in all His glory. Thank Jesus for eternal life!

I would like to quote something not found in the Bible, but rather in a Christian song book. Notice that the song starts out with the words "Praise God" and "Praise Him." The context is singular meaning ONE. The words of the song end with "Praise Father, Son, and Holy Ghost." The context this time is plural meaning THREE. Three Persons equal the one GOD! Praise them equally!

DOXOLOGY

"Praise God, from whom all blessings flow; praise Him, all creatures here below; Praise Him above, ye heavenly host; Praise Father, Son, and Holy Ghost! Amen."

A bumper sticker I saw on a car says it well. "NO JESUS, NO LIFE. KNOW JESUS, KNOW LIFE!

I do know that we can have a personal relationship with God. We can choose to love God, because God chose to love us, even before we were born. He will express that love to us throughout eternity in ways that we cannot even begin to comprehend. I believe we will never, never, ever cease to be continually amazed by God's love. And as for this glorious eternity that He has planned for those of us who have accepted eternal life (forgiveness and unconditional love) in Jesus Christ, don't expect even one dull moment. Do expect paradise beyond everyone's imagination.

I hope the message of this book has helped you understand how eternally important Jesus is and...*who* He is. Jesus asked these questions:

> "Who do men say that I, the Son of man, am?"
> —Matt. 16:13

> "Who do the crowds say that I am?"
> —Luke 9:18

And then Jesus asked that same question directly to you and me.

> "But who do **you** say that I am?"
> —Mark 8:29

> Now when He (Jesus) had spoken these things, while they watched, He was taken up, and a cloud received Him out of their sight. And while they looked steadfastly toward heaven as He went up, behold two men in white apparel (angles), who also said, "Men of Galilee, why do you stand gazing up into heaven? This same Jesus, who was taken up from you into heaven, will so come in like manner as you saw Him go into heaven."
> —Acts 1:9-11

Encourage one another with these words. **Jesus is coming again!**

Visit the "am I who I am" Web site at:
www.amiwhoiam.com
or e-mail questions & comments to:
philip@amiwhoiam.com

Printed in the United States
215836BV00001B/3/P

9 781414 109060